USING THE XBOX 360
AS A STIMULUS FOR LITERACY

CREATIVE EDUCATIONAL PRESS LTD

PUBLISHED BY: Creative Educational Press Ltd
2 The Walled Garden
Grange Park Drive
Biddulph
Staffs
ST8 7TA
Tel: 07789 938923
Fax: 01782 379398

PRINTED BY: York Publishing Services
64 Hallfield Road
Layerthorpe
York
YO31 7ZQ

Alan Peat   www.alanpeat.com
info@alanpeat.com

Simon Matthews   www.s2air.co.uk
info@s2air.co.uk

ISBN: 978-0-9544755-6-7

Also available from Creative Educational Press Ltd: (www.thecepress.com)
50 Ways To Retell A Story: Cinderella by Alan Peat, Julie Peat and Chris Storey
Get Your Head Around Punctuation (... And how to teach it!) by Alan Peat
Writing Exciting Sentences: Age 7 Plus by Alan Peat
Writing Exciting Ghost Stories: Ghost Story Plot Skeletons: Age 9 Plus by Alan Peat (co-author Julie Barnfather)

Other titles by Alan Peat available through Creative Educational Press Ltd (www.thecepress.com)
Teaching Poetry with 4-8 year olds (Imaginative Minds Publishing)
Teaching Poetry with 7-12 year olds (Imaginative Minds Publishing)
Word Games at Key Stage 2 (Nash Pollock Publishing)
Improving Story Writing KS 1 &2 (Nash Pollock Publishing)
Improving Non-Fiction Writing KS 1 & 2 (co-written with Margaret McNeil) (Nash Pollock Publishing)

Design: Simon Matthews

USING THE XBOX 360

AS A STIMULUS FOR LITERACY

RUSSELL NEWMAN

Acknowledgements

The author wishes to thank these people for their efforts in helping to create this book: Ian, Naomi, James, Graham, Ruth, Emma, Mark S, Mark J, Sarah, Clare, Vera, Andrew, Catherine, Nathan.

The staff and pupils of:

Pinfold Street J.M.I. School

St. Francis Xavier Catholic Primary School

Moorcroft Wood Primary School

St. Peter's Catholic Primary School

Shireland Hall Primary School

Thanks also to Julie, Simon and Alan for their dedication to the project and their support.

This book is dedicated to Nayra.

DISCLAIMER: All the demos used as resources in this book were available from the Xbox 360 Marketplace at the time of printing. The author and publishers of this book have no control over the Marketplace or the removal of any of the demos and therefore cannot be held responsible for any of this book's chapters becoming obsolete owing to the subsequent removal of a demo.

Contents

Writing is a stubborn problem in many of our schools and doing more of what we are already doing (in such a context) is unlikely to alter this situation.

What is needed is a range of divergent strategies which motivate pupils to engage in the writing process. The integration of games consoles and literacy development is one such divergent strategy worthy of consideration.

In this book by Russell Newman, the Xbox 360 console is used as the starting point for a broad range of engaging writing activities. Russell draws on his own personal interest and experience as both a teacher and deputy headteacher in order to produce a book which will prove an invaluable tool in the drive to raise writing standards.

Teachers in the UK have been quick to embrace the enhanced learning opportunities which ICT affords, with computers and interactive whiteboards now being seen as essential learning tools. Yet gaming consoles are still often perceived as domestic products with limited application in the school environment.

This position is slowly altering. Teachers just entering the profession have been surrounded by digital, information and communication technology since birth and those of us who are 'longer in the tooth' cannot fail to recognise the enthusiasm for 'gaming' which undoubtedly exists – our high streets bear testament to this!

Using computer games as a stimulus for writing activities has several key benefits:

1. Pupil perceptions of literacy are enhanced – children enjoy computer games!

2. VAK (Visual, Auditory and Kinaesthetic) balance learning situations are facilitated – computer games can lead to an 'immersive' learning experience.

3. A computer game is less threatening than a blank sheet of paper.

4. Many games offer cross-curricular learning opportunities.

In 2009, US President Barack Obama announced the 'Educate to Innovate' campaign, focusing on the development of new computer games which are being designed specifically with the purpose of interesting pupils in science and maths. The American Entertainment Software Association is a key player in this project and its president, Michael Gallagher, recently (2009) said: "Computer and video games are one of the most effective ways to reach America's children and encourage them to stay interested... "

While the American campaign aims to foster a greater national focus on science, technology, engineering and maths (STEM), its principles are equally applicable to literacy development in the UK.

We trust that this book will prove to be an invaluable tool in the (hard!) drive to raise writing standards.

Alan Peat

Setting up the Xbox 360
for use in the classroom
Important- Please refer to the manual in the Xbox 360 console box for first set-up.

This guide is designed for teachers who need to set up the console for use in the classroom. **All demos will need to have been downloaded previously from the Xbox Live Marketplace using a home internet point. See page 6.**

This set-up has been tested with different projectors; however it cannot be guaranteed that every projector will set up in the same way. The Xbox 360 comes packaged with a SCART adaptor that can be used to plug the Xbox 360 into a television if the projector is unavailable*.

This is all the equipment you will need to set up the Xbox 360:

1.   Xbox 360 console (the hard disk is located on the top of the console)
2.   Audio/Visual HD component cable
3.   SCART Adaptor
4.   Xbox 360 wireless controller (An additional controller may be used for the FIFA 10 activities, and is purchased separately.)
5.   Power cord and power supply
6.   (Not pictured) projector or television

This was true at the time of publication.

Connecting the Xbox 360 to the projector or television

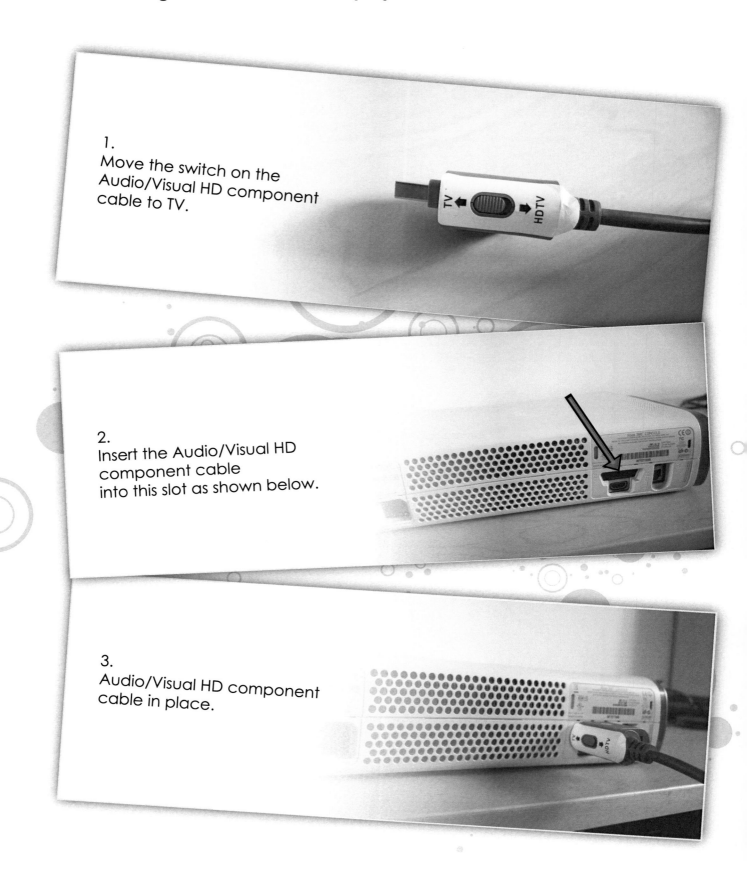

1.
Move the switch on the Audio/Visual HD component cable to TV.

2.
Insert the Audio/Visual HD component cable into this slot as shown below.

3.
Audio/Visual HD component cable in place.

4.
These 3 wires on the other end of the Audio/Visual HD component cable will need to be connected to the projector.

Red and white = Audio
Yellow = Visual

5.
Many projectors will have clear labels for inserting additional inputs. The yellow wire will need to go in the socket labelled *Video In* (this is normally coloured yellow).

The red and white wires will need to go into the *Audio In* sockets. (These are normally coloured red and/or white.)*

6.
Alternatively, the Xbox 360 can be attached directly to a television. To do this, insert the red, white and yellow wires into the SCART adaptor as shown. This can then be inserted into the vast majority of televisions.

Projectors will vary; consult the individual manual for complete instructions.

Connecting the Xbox 360 to the power supply

7.
The power supply (illustration 5 on page 1) should have a normal wall plug on one end and the connector for the Xbox 360 (as shown in the picture) on the other. Both ends are essential for powering the console.

8.
The power supply needs to be inserted into the Xbox 360 console as shown below.

9.
The Xbox 360 power supply correctly inserted.

At this point the power plug can be inserted into a power point.

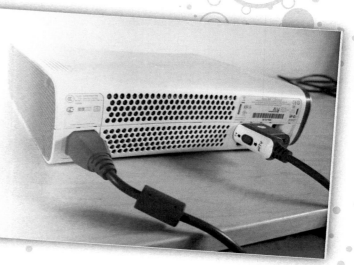

Turning the Xbox 360 on

10.
Press the large circle located on the right-hand side of the front of the Xbox 360 console. The outer ring will light up green.

11.
Press and hold the central X button on the Xbox 360 wireless controller and it will also light up green. This shows that it is connected to the Xbox.

(To insert and remove batteries please follow the Xbox 360 manual provided.)*

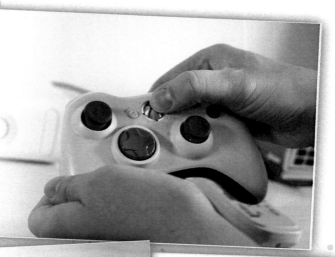

12.
(Projector controllers will vary.)

Press video on the projector controller and this will now show the Xbox 360 starting screen. Volume may need to be adjusted on the projector also.

The mute button on some projector controllers is also effective as it will mute both picture and sound and can be a useful tool when delivering the activities.

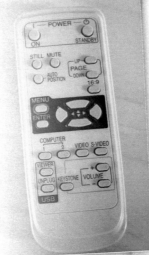

To turn off the Xbox, hold down the centre 'X' button on the Xbox 360 wireless controller until an option screen comes up on screen. Move the left direction stick to turn off console and press A.

*The wireless control pad will come packaged with 2 AA batteries. Over time these batteries will need to be replaced. A Play and Charge kit can be purchased which will allow the controller to be recharged without the need for continuous use of batteries. Follow the instructions for use that come with the product.

How to download the demos to your Xbox 360 console

NOTE: The demos you require for this book can be found only by downloading them from Microsoft's Xbox Live service. This will need to be completed only once per Xbox. You do not need to repeat this process once the demos are downloaded.

You will need:

- Xbox 360 hard disk drive: either 20gb, 60gb or 120gb or a USB storage device with at least 4gb of memory

- A broadband internet connection

NOTE: Many Local Authorities prevent access to downloadable materials in school for security. The demos will be easiest to download at home. The Xbox needs to be connected to the internet via the Ethernet cable that comes with the console. See documentation regarding this in the Xbox manual.

- A Windows Live email address (e.g. hotmail)

Visit www.hotmail.com to sign up for a free email account if not already registered. You may wish to create a school-based one to use for this:

e.g. Yourschool@hotmail.com

Setting up an Xbox Live Account

When the Xbox is turned on for the first time, you will need to follow the on-screen instructions for its initial set up. Once this has been completed you will have the option of signing up for Xbox live. Press A on the 'Yes, join Xbox Live' section of the screen and follow the guidance given.

NOTE: When completing this process, the Ethernet cable must be connected to the Xbox and your broadband router (individual routers may vary; consult your manual for support). If you want to connect the console wirelessly*, there are wireless network adaptors available from around £40 (pictured opposite). The Xbox may download updates at this time and this is normal. Please do not turn off the console when instructed not to.

The sign-up process for Xbox Live is simple to follow on screen. You will need to provide details to create an account, starting with the email address you wish to use.

Once the email address has been entered and verified, you will be prompted to choose a subscription plan. The gold subscription is not required to access the demos of the games. So choose the bottom option: 'I don't want a gold membership'.

You will then be offered a free month-trial of Xbox live. However, this requires payment details. So choose the 'No, add it later' option.

After this you will be prompted to add any other information needed to set up an account. Again, you may wish to use school details when setting up an account.

The next screens will give further customisation choices regarding Xbox Live. Read each stage carefully. Note that the gamer tag name chosen may be school-related.

NOTE: As many pupils will be knowledgeable about using Xbox Live, and its systems of communications (e.g. messaging), it may be wise not to share the gamer tag information with pupils!

The next step is to create an avatar (an on-screen representation of the owner of the Xbox). This part may be skipped by selecting one of the example avatars and choosing 'Save and Exit' at the bottom of the screen by pressing A.

Accessing and downloading the demos

You will now be on the Xbox 'Dashboard' (you will see this every time you turn on the console). By moving the left directional stick up and down you can cycle through the different channels of the dashboard.

Find the 'Game Marketplace' section of the dashboard, then press A on 'Explore Game Content'. Next you will see a similar screen to the dashboard. Press A on the 'Browse' panel of the 'All Games' section.

At this stage you will be presented with an alphabetical list which can quickly be accessed for each game. Press A to choose the game once you can see it on screen. You will then be given a list of options regarding the game. Choose 'Get Demo' by pressing A. Then confirm download by again pressing A.

At this point you can download all of the demos by following this process again.

The games required and (download sizes) are:

Demo	File Size
FIFA 10	979.43 MB
Kameo, Elements of Power	1.01 GB (1000 MB)
Thrillville, Off The Rails	331.07 MB
Viva Pinata, Trouble in Paradise	1.52 GB (1500MB)

NOTE: Please be aware that downloading these demos will take time (varying lengths depending on your internet speed) and may also impact on your fair usage policy with your internet service provider. It is recommended that you consult your internet Service Provider before downloading large files.

The games will then be stored on the Xbox hard disk drive or USB storage device to be used at any time.

The latest iteration of the Xbox 360 now includes built-in wireless capabilities.

FIFA 10

Synopsis

FIFA 10 is the 2010 edition of the long-running football series by EA sports. The game benefits from having full licensing and approval for use of player likenesses for most of the world's major leagues.

The game is released every year and while there are subtle changes in game play and features, the core mechanic has been very similar in the past few years, and is in the following games in the series.

The demo of the game allows two players (up to a total of 4) to play a game which runs for six minutes. The teams available are:

Chelsea*
Bayern Munchen*
Barcelona *
Juventus*
OM
Chicago Fire

*Lists of player names and positions for the first team are available. The available teams have been chosen owing to the familiarity that many children already have with these football teams.

There are demos of the previous games (including FIFA 09) which are also in the series, and demos will undoubtedly be available for future games.

Controls in Game
(Full controls can be accessed from the pause menu in game. Press Start, then move the left directional stick down to match options and move the stick left. Move the stick down to Xbox 360 controller settings.)

With the ball (Attacking)

LOB PASS/CROSS/HEADER

THROUGH BALL

MOVE PLAYER

SHOOT/VOLLEY/HEADER

SHORT PASS/HEADER

PAUSE GAME

SLOW DRIBBLE WITH BALL

PLAYER SPRINT

Controls in Game (cont.)
Without the ball (Defending)

SLIDING TACKLE

CLEARANCE

MOVE PLAYER

CLEARANCE

STANDING TACKLE

PAUSE GAME

CHANGE PLAYER

PLAYER SPRINT

Other controls are available; however, these are the basic controls necessary for a pupil to play the game comfortably.

Team: Barcelona

Position		Shirt Number	Name
GK	(Goalkeeper	1	V. Valdes
RB	(Right back)	2	D. Alves
RCB	(Right centre back)	5	C. Puyol
LCB	(Left centre back)	3	G. Piqué
LB	(Left back)	22	E. Abidal
RCM	(Right central midfielder)	6	Xavi Hernandez
CM	(Central midfielder)	24	Y. Toure
LCM	(Left central midfielder)	19	A. Iniesta
RW	(Right-winger)	10	L. Messi
ST	(Striker)	9	Z. Ibrahimović
LW	(Left-winger)	14	T. Henry

Team: Bayern Munchen

Position		Shirt Number	Name
GK	(Goalkeeper)	1	M. Rensing
RB	(Right back)	21	P. Lahm
RCB	(Right centre back)	5	D. Van Buyten
LCB	(Left centre back)	28	H. Badstuber
LB	(Left back)	23	D. Pranjić
RM	(Right midfielder)	8	H. Altintop
CDM	(Central defensive midfielder)	17	M. Van Bommel
LM	(Left midfielder)	31	B. Schweinsteiger
CAM	(Central attacking midfielder)	7	F. Ribéry
RS	(Right striker)	33	M. Gomec
LS	(Left striker)	18	M. Klose

Team: Juventus

Position		Shirt Number	Name
GK	(Goalkeeper)	1	G. Buffon
RB	(Right back)	21	Z. Grygera
RCB	(Right centre back)	5	F. Cannavaro
LCB	(Left centre back)	3	G. Chiellini
LB	(Left back)	19	C. Molinaro
CDM	(Central defensive midfielder)	4	F. Melo
RM	(Right midfielder)	16	M. Camoranesi
LM	(Left midfielder)	22	M. Sissoko
CAM	(Central attacking midfielder)	28	Diego Ribas
RS	(Right striker)	11	Amauri Carvalho
LS	(Left striker)	10	A. Del Piero

Team: Chelsea

Position		Shirt Number	Name
GK	(Goalkeeper)	1	P. Cech
RB	(Right back)	17	J. Bosingwa
RCB	(Right centre back)	6	R. Carvalho
LCB	(Left centre back)	26	J. Terry
LB	(Left back)	3	A. Cole
CDM	(Central defensive midfielder)	12	J. Obi Mikel
RM	(Right midfielder)	5	M. Essien
LM	(Left midfielder)	15	F. Malouda
CAM	(Central attacking midfielder)	8	F. Lampard
RS	(Right striker)	39	N. Anelka
LS	(Left striker)	11	D. Drogba

Activity One: To develop note-making skills with FIFA 10

Target/s

To improve and develop note-making, using FIFA 10 as a live stimulus

How long?

Each game on the demo lasts 6 minutes.
Activity 40 minutes

Equipment

◎ Xbox 360 console (including Hard Disk Drive)

◎ FIFA 10 Demo (needs to be downloaded before the lesson from the Xbox Live Marketplace)

◎ An additional Xbox 360 controller (for 2 player games)

◎ Projector

◎ Activity Sheet: Developing note-making skills with FIFA 10 (See below.)

Group size

Whole-class activity (working in pairs)

Concept

The use of a sporting situation provides children with a dynamic stimulus for note-making, an important skill which is notoriously difficult to teach in a stimulating manner. In addition, the fact that the action is controlled by fellow pupils adds an extra sense of ownership and immersion to the activity. Note-making in this scenario also lends itself to journalistic/recount writing.

Game set-up

◎ Follow instructions for setting-up the Xbox 360 as shown on pages 2 - 4.

◎ Turn the Xbox 360 on.

◎ Under 'My Xbox', scroll right to 'Games Library' using the left directional stick.

◎ Press A. (The game demos should appear on the 'Recent Games' list.)

◎ Scroll down using the left directional stick to the FIFA 10 demo.

◎ Press Y with the demo selected and it will load automatically.

◎ Press start when prompted. When the screen shows a footballer on a football pitch, press start again to access the menu.

◎ Choose *English, Beginner* and *Classic Controls* by pressing A when prompted.

◎ When the screen shows a footballer on a football pitch, press start to access the menu.

◎ Press A on kick-off.

◎ Press A on Exhibition match.

◎ If two players are present, player two will need to be moved to the left side of the screen with the left directional stick. Press A to advance.

◎ Each child chooses a team by moving the left directional stick left or right. Press A when ready.

◎ Choose a kit by moving the left directional stick left or right. Press A when chosen.

◎ Press A on *Play Match*.

◎ When game has loaded, it will instruct players to press start (bottom left corner of the screen).

Instant replay instructions

To watch instant replays at any time during the game, pause the game by pressing start and move the left directional stick down to instant replay and press A. The commands available to you are shown on screen:

Command button	Action
Left trigger	Rewind
Right trigger	Fast forward
A button	Play/ Pause
X button	Change camera view
Right/ Left Bumper	Change target player (Player the replay focuses in upon.)

Replays will show the last 10 seconds of action. Each goal scored will receive its own individual replay.

Activity

Explain to the children that they are going to be making notes from a live football match. Discuss and reinforce what note-making means, and strategies for effective note-making. Decide on clear success criteria, which will be based on the ability of the class/group.

Teachers may wish to reinforce/establish the following key points about note-making:

◎ Use of abbreviations for speed of note-making e.g. Wayne Rooney = WR

◎ Making notes only on important information/events

◎ Use of simple words and phrases instead of elongated sentences

◎ Use of bullet points/dashes/sections to organise notes effectively

Modelling this activity by using a computer-controlled game while the teacher acts as scribe would be a useful way of sharing expectations with the children. To access a computer versus computer match:

○ On the team-select screen, slide the controller icons (by using the left directional stick) into the centre space. The game will ask you if you wish to proceed without nominated human-controlled players. Just press A button on 'yes'.

After modelling the concept, invite two children to take part in the game. Follow the instructions as laid out above. While the game is underway, pupils will need to make notes on events occurring during the game. This activity can be supported using the photocopiable activity sheet overleaf. During the game the action can be paused for key events (e.g. near misses). This is important as it allows the children to spend more time on important events in the game. To use the instant replay function, pause the game and follow the instructions above.

With a demo time limit of six minutes (90 in-game minutes), children will have only a brief amount of time to focus on the game which will allow for more concentrated note-making. If the game is level at the end of 90 minutes, penalties are used to decide the game.

When the match is over, the game automatically selects and displays the important action. This provides children with a benchmark by which to judge whether or not any key events were missed. In addition, statistics for the game are displayed and can be used to develop notes.

As a class, discuss the notes that have been made and what the key events were. Bring together all of the children's ideas and create a whole-class set of notes based upon the game. While compiling the notes as a class, model how to effectively edit these. When completed, these notes can then be used in further work such as journalistic writing.

-------------------- Match timeline --------------------

Teams: v	1 min- 22 mins	23mins- 45 mins	46 mins- 67 mins	68 mins- 90 mins	Penalties (If game is level at 90 mins)
Key events Who? What?					
Score	..	..	..	..	..
Scorers Who?					

Activity Two: To develop concise oral reporting and to improve use of positional language using FIFA 10

Target/s

To commentate on a football match using clear reporting and developing a variety of positional language

How long?

Each game on the demo lasts 6 minutes
Activity 10 minutes

Equipment

◎ Xbox 360 console (including Hard Disk Drive)

◎ FIFA 10 Demo (needs to be downloaded before the lesson from the Xbox Live Marketplace)

◎ An additional Xbox 360 controller (for 2 player games)

◎ Projector

◎ Sky sports news website http://www.skysports.com/football

◎ Radio Five Live website http://www.bbc.co.uk/fivelive/

◎ Microphone or sound recorder

Group size

Groups of 2-4. It will be necessary for children to attempt this in small groups and, as such, the rest of the class will need a separate task.

Concept

By commentating upon a live event, children will develop the need to be clear and concise in their reporting. Also, manipulating this familiar football setting into a speaking and listening activity allows children to gain reporting confidence. Furthermore, this activity will help children to use positional language effectively in their future writing.

Game set-up

◎ Follow instructions for setting-up the Xbox 360 as shown on page 2 - 4.

◎ Follow 'Game set-up' instructions as shown on page 15.

Instant replay instructions

To watch instant replays at any time during the game, pause the game by pressing start and move the left directional stick down to instant replay and press A. The commands available to you are shown on screen as well as on pages 9 and 10. Replays will show the last 10 seconds of action. Each goal scored will receive its own individual replay.

Activity

Explain to the children that they will be creating a commentary based upon a match from FIFA 10. Share a clip of a match commentary*. Discuss with the children how best to report on live action:

◎ the need for clear, precise vocabulary;

◎ positional language to describe the action accurately;

◎ precision linked to attempts to maintain interest of the listener.

Explore the varied vocabulary and expressions used by professional commentators. To aid this discussion the 'Commentating Vocabulary' sheet (p22) provides some examples of football vocabulary. The list is not exhaustive and can be expanded by pupils. Ask questions about the words: can any of the words/phrases be used in other sports or other reporting situations? While listening to a commentary, encourage pupils to make a note of any positional language used:

◎ 'He swept the ball across the pitch towards the forward player.'

Opposite on *Activity Sheet Two* there are examples of positional language for children to use when commentating on the game.

For the activity, the children will need to be seated in a position where they can comfortably see all of the action. The game will be played by computer-controlled characters; the children will watch and report live on the events of the game as they unfold. In order to assess the speaking and listening objective, teachers may wish to use recording equipment to capture what the children say. This would create an opportunity to present the activity to the class for evaluation by peers.

Recording options include using a PC microphone and the sound recorder software, or a tape/memory card sound recorder.

Pupils, in pairs or small groups, will then report on the game. While the activity is underway, constant reinforcement of the important features of commentary is necessary so that it can form a purposeful starting point for future report writing.

When the activity is completed and recordings have been made, allow the children to listen to their reports. This will provide an important self-evaluation opportunity.

*Use http://www.skysports.com/football to find examples of commentary.

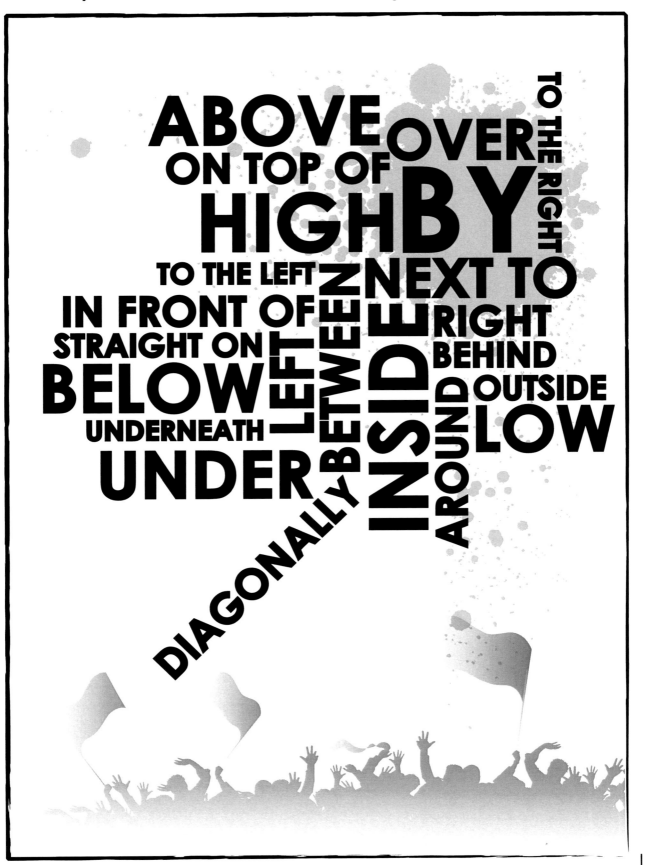

Strike Score Goal
Corner Referee Fans
Slide tackle Chance Pass
Red card Yellow card Save
Open goal Offside Crossbar
Whistle Challenge Header
Free kick Throw in Injury
Crowd Player Football
Penalty Kick off Foul

Activity Three: To use role play to develop questioning and interviewing skills using FIFA 10

Target/s

To use varied questions to elicit detailed responses about events in a football game

To develop empathy with key characters in a sporting setting (using FIFA 10 demo)

How long?

Each game on the demo lasts 6 minutes.
Activity 45 minutes

Equipment

◎ Xbox 360 console (including Hard Disk Drive)

◎ FIFA 10 Demo (needs to be downloaded before the lesson from the Xbox Live Marketplace)

◎ An additional Xbox 360 controller (for 2 player games)

◎ Projector

◎ Sky sports news website http://www.skysports.com/football

◎ Radio Five Live website http://www.bbc.co.uk/fivelive/

◎ Microphone or sound recorder

Group size

Whole-class activity (working in groups)

Concept

In this activity, some children will have the opportunity to take on the role of key players from the match. Other children will be encouraged to develop questioning skills to gain additional information that can be used in future report/journalistic writing. By taking on roles from the game, children develop empathy towards characters in a more engaging context than many role-play scenarios.

Game set-up

◎ Follow instructions for setting up the Xbox 360 as shown on page 2 - 4.

◎ Follow 'Game set-up' instructions as shown on page 15.

Instant replay instructions

To watch instant replays at any time during the game, pause the game by pressing start. Then move the left directional stick down to *instant replay* and press A. The commands available to you are shown on screen as well as on pages 9 and 10. Replays will show the last 10 seconds of action. Each goal scored will receive its own individual replay.

Activity

Ask pupils how journalists gather information. Establish that interviews are a key factor, and that responses to interviewing add meaningful detail to a report. Explain to the pupils that they are going to be taking on the role of the key characters at a sporting event. Using the FIFA 10 Demo, allow two pupils to take the roles of the two teams and play the game. During the four minutes of game time, encourage the other pupils to make brief notes about any key events in the game that can be explored with the players after the game (e.g. goals, saves). Notes can be structured using the note-making frame from activity one. (p18)

When the game is over, use the replay feature to explore the key action in the games. As a class, decide which characters should be interviewed post-match. This discussion is important, as it encourages children to identify and prioritise key players in a scene. Tip: Questions directed towards a manager will be different from those directed towards a player; a victorious player will be asked different questions from a defeated player.

Any member of the class may take on the roles of the chosen characters from the game. After a decision has been made as to which characters will be interviewed, pupils then need to create a list of questions (in groups) to ask the characters. Examples of types of characters that could be chosen include:

◎ goal scorers;

◎ managers;

◎ goalkeepers;

◎ star players.

Before starting the task, ensure that pupils have a clear understanding of the range of questions that can be asked and the advantages/disadvantages of each:

◎ Open questioning: Questions that require the character to answer in detail (e.g. How did you feel when you scored the goal?)

◎ Closed questioning: Questions that may receive simple answers (e.g. How many shots did you have in the game?)

At this stage it may be worth watching a post-match interview. The Sky Sports website, Radio Five Live website* or any other suitable news clip involving interviewing can be used to provide a working model .

The first activity sheet provided may be used by the children to jot down their questions. (Share effective examples as the activity progresses.) The quantity and type of these 'model' questions can be modified to cater for different ability groups. In addition, children may use the 'question words' sheet (p.27) to vary the openings of their questions, thereby gaining different responses.

After the groups have compiled a list of questions, invite pupils to volunteer to come to the front of the class and adopt the role of the chosen characters from the game. You may wish to use props to fully engage the selected pupils (such as goalkeeper gloves, football shirt and suits/jacket).

* http://www.skysports.com/football
  http://www.bbc.co.uk/fivelive/

Pupils then take turns to question the role-player. Tip: pupils can write the responses on the activity sheet provided. This reinforces the previous note-making activity. These responses may form the basis of subsequent report writing.

Provide feedback to the pupils who take on the roles and also to those asking questions. All children taking part in the activity should be praised: as in any other drama situation, self-confidence is vital.

Extension

To stretch higher ability groups, pupils could be split into two different sets of interviewers - one for each team. This ensures that the pupils who are creating questions also have the opportunity to take on a role.

This approach may be developed so that the concept of 'bias' is considered. With selected questions, the teacher could illustrate the effect of positive and negative questioning, and how the tone and insinuation of questions can depend on the bias of the questioner.

Activity Three:
To use role play to develop questioning and interviewing skills

Question Number	Question	Response
1		
2		
3		
4		
5		

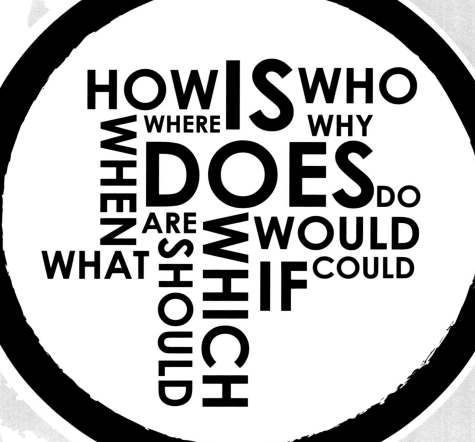

Activity Four: To write a journalistic report using FIFA 10

Target/s

To use FIFA 10 as a stimulus for writing a journalistic report

To produce a creative piece of journalistic writing

How long?

Each game on the demo lasts 6 minutes.
Activity 45 - 60 minutes

Equipment

◎ Xbox 360 console (including Hard Disk Drive)

◎ FIFA 10 Demo (needs to be downloaded before the lesson from the Xbox Live Marketplace)

◎ An additional Xbox 360 controller (for 2 player games)

◎ Projector

◎ Sky sports news website http://www.skysports.com/football

◎ Radio Five Live website http://www.bbc.co.uk/fivelive/

Group size

Whole-class activity

Concept

By using FIFA 10 as the stimulus, pupils are encouraged to report carefully on a sporting event. If this lesson follows the previous activities created for this game, a complete and focused piece of journalistic writing, with concrete relevance for pupils, can be achieved.

Game set-up

◎ Follow instructions for setting up the Xbox 360 as shown on page 2 - 4.

◎ Follow 'Game set-up' instructions as shown on page 15.

Instant replay instructions

To watch instant replays at any time during the game, pause the game by pressing start and move the left directional stick down to instant replay and press A. The commands available to you are shown on screen as well as on page 9 and 10. Replays will show the last 10 seconds of action. Each goal scored will receive its own individual replay.

Activity

Before attempting this activity, pupils will need an understanding of the structure, style and language features of journalistic writing. As such, before writing, it is necessary for pupils to explore and deconstruct real journalistic reports (you may wish to use the *Sky Sports* website).

Share the objective - writing a journalistic report using FIFA 10 - with the children. Allow pupils time to discuss what they think the features of an effective journalistic report are. Share views, and create success criteria based on both pupil & teacher inputs.

POINTS TO CONSIDER:

◎ Simple structure: Headline, opening paragraph, main body of the text, quotations, final concluding paragraph- which may bring the article back to present tense

◎ Short paragraphs and short sentences for concision

◎ 3rd person throughout

◎ Factual, yet descriptive language used for effect

◎ Direct and reported speech used to expand details found in the report.

Once the success criteria have been discussed and shared, play the demo and encourage pupils to make notes for the journalistic piece of writing. Rather than having two children playing the game, you may wish to have all children making notes. If this is the case:

◎ Instead of each child choosing a team, move both controller icons to the centre of the screen and press A to continue. The game will ask if you would like to advance without selecting a side. Move the left directional stick to yes and press A. The computer will then play as both teams.

The note-making sheet from Activity One may be used to help pupils to compose their notes. When the game is complete, the computer will generate a short replay of the match. This can be left on screen throughout the activity as an aid. At half-time and full-time, a range of statistics is displayed which can aid the report.

Pupils can then spend time focusing upon the key journalistic question-stems:

◎ Who?

◎ Where?

◎ What?

◎ When?

◎ Why?

◎ How?

The activity sheet on page 31 may be used to this end.

When pupils have had time to make notes on the events and add them to their plan, they should be encouraged to create a journalistic report based upon the whole match. Remind pupils of the need for direct and reported speech (the role-play activity would be an excellent development tool for this aspect of journalistic writing). While the writing is underway, constant reinforcement of the success criteria will provide pupils with an embedded understanding of the key features.

When the reports are completed, pupils should be encouraged to self-evaluate their work against the success criteria. Peer evaluation will also be effective.

To extend a higher ability group, pupils could be given specific newspapers to report for (either tabloid or broadsheet).

This would lead to an understanding of the differing stylistic approaches taken by tabloid and broadsheet newspapers.

Extension

To extend this activity, the report could be recorded as a radio broadcast or podcast thereby developing the initial work for a different medium. (See websites from the 'Equipment List' on page 28 for examples of sports broadcasts.)

Podcast creation is relatively simple, requiring only a microphone and some voice-recording software such as 'Audacity' which is freely available from:

audacity.sourceforge.net

For further information on creating your own podcast visit:

www.ilounge.com/index.php/articles/comments/beginners-guide-to-podcast-creation

Who?	
Where?	
What?	
When?	
Why?	
How?	

Pupil Examples: FIFA 10

Issy, St. Peter's Catholic Primary School, West Midlands

FIFA 2010 note-taking sheet

Match timeline →

Teams: Chelsea V Barcelona	1min – 22mins	23 mins – 45 mins	46 mins – 67 mins	68 mins – 90 mins	Penalties If the game is a tie after 90 minutes
Key events Who? What?	A shoots, misses free kick. 12 mins in by Terry D.D Shoots, misses.	Messi runs out Xani takes corner. No goals 2 shoots on each team. No yellow or red cards	T.H shoots, misses. Zobi shot come off keeper headed out. Messi missed.	Bar shots, misses. Free kick by Chelsea, B got yellow card.	Lampard missed. Messi scored. F.M scored T.M scored Anelka scored. Xani scored M.E scored A.1 missed. Cole scored.
Score	0 : 0	0 : 0	0 : 0	0 : 0	4 : 3
Scorers: Who?					Chelsea

Activity Three:
To use role play to develop questioning
and interviewing skills

Question Number	Question	Response
1 Emma Jamie	What would you say your team needs to improve on?	There skills for golas and there free kicks.
2 Emma Jamie	What would you give you team out of Ten?	$9\frac{1}{2}$ out of Ten because There is still parts they need to work on.
3 Emma Alex	How do you think your team played?	Very well but like I said there is still parts that need to be improved.
4 Emma Alex	How do you think your team shoud play in the next Match?	I hope they will do as well as today but Like I said there is still parts to improve on but very other than that.
5 Saskia Olivia	When did you have dought your team might loose?	At the Start but they pulled it back, So well done to them.

Synopsis

Thrillville: Off The Rails is a theme-park simulation game, created by LucasArts, in which players assume the role of a theme park manager. The demo allows for a small section of a theme park to be used in a variety of different ways:

- Players can add or remove rides from the park.

- All rides are fully interactive and can be used by the pupils.

The setting for the demo is a theme-park called Throttleville, a stunt themed park in a desert setting.

The suggested activities encompass a variety of genres and teaching opportunities. They can therefore be used as a revision tool, or as discrete lessons linked to appropriate blocked units of study.

Controls in Game

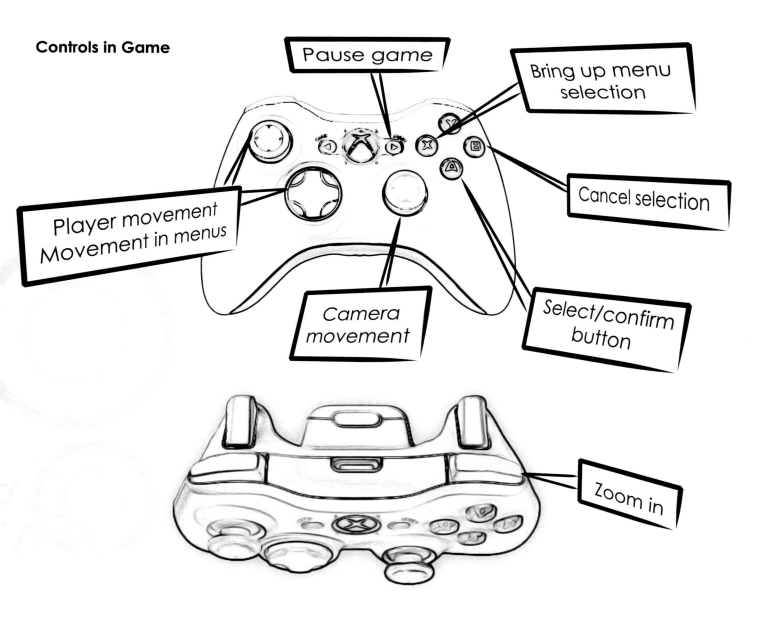

Pause game

Bring up menu selection

Player movement
Movement in menus

Cancel selection

Camera movement

Select/confirm button

Zoom in

Most of the events in the game are triggered by using the A button. In the bottom corner of the screen there is a small circle which turns green and shows the letter A when there is something the player can interact with.

Other buttons may be used under certain circumstances. Where this occurs, the buttons needed are shown on screen for reference.

Activity Five: To use persuasive language to advertise the Throttleville theme park

Target/s

To describe a location effectively, using a broad range of descriptive language

To use persuasive language concisely for maximum effect

How long?

60 minutes

Equipment

- Xbox 360 console (including Hard Disk Drive)

- *Thrilleville: Off the Rails* Demo (needs to be downloaded before the lesson from the Xbox Live Marketplace)

- Projector

- Recording device *e.g. voice recorder or video camera*

Group size

Whole-class activity (working in pairs)

Concept

This game allows the player to explore a small theme park in a desert setting which will be unfamiliar to the majority of pupils. Pupils can take turns on each ride, engaging them deeply with work based upon the game. The graphics are colourful and there is a wide variety of activities occurring around the park. Pupils are encouraged to observe and describe these. Pupils then use their descriptions to create a radio advertisement, persuading people to visit Throttleville. This advertisement can then be recorded and played back for self, peer and teacher assessment.

Game set-up

- Follow instructions for setting up the Xbox 360 as shown on page 2 - 4.

- Turn the Xbox 360 on.

- Under 'My Xbox', scroll right to 'Games Library' using the left directional stick.

- Press A. (The game demos should appear on the 'Recent Games' list.)

- Scroll down using the left directional stick to the *Thrillville: OTR* demo.

- Press Y with the demo selected and it will load automatically.

- Press start when prompted.

- Press A on 'New Game'. (At this point the game will allow you to choose a character and select name, appearance and clothing. This is an area that can be bypassed, as it is not necessary for any of the activities in this book.)

- When the character is chosen, move down using the left directional stick to start game and press A. After this, a short video plays in which the professor who creates rides for the game introduces himself. This can be skipped by pressing Start.

- Keep pressing A to skip through the next instructions.

- From this point on, the character is free to be controlled by the player.

Activity

In pairs, ask pupils to make a list of five (or more) words to describe a theme park. Make a list of these words so they can be seen throughout the lesson. This list acts as a 'working document' to which new words and phrases can subsequently be added (by pupils and/or staff). When a suitable number of words has been added to the list, explain to the pupils that they are going to explore a brand-new theme park.

Before beginning the exploration, the pupils need to be aware of success criteria for describing the theme park ...

What can they see? Colours, shapes, sizes etc.

What can they hear? People, rides, sound effects, radio etc.

Imagine how they might feel. How does it feel to be in the desert? What is it like to be on the rides?

Imagine what the location would smell like. What foods are on sale? There will be smoke from the vehicles etc.

Imagine what they might taste at the theme park. What are the most tasty foods/drinks/sweets?

All rides can be accessed by just walking up to them using the left directional stick and pressing A. During a ride the camera will take on a first-person view as the ride begins. The viewpoint can be changed using the Y button. Teachers may wish to invite pupils to control the character for short periods of time, thereby allowing large numbers to experience the game. During the exploration, pupils can, in pairs or groups, write down words and phrases to describe the theme park.

Children can fully explore the rides (there are four at the start of the demo and more can be added.) Suggest suitable descriptive sentences, and ask pupils controlling characters to pause at different locations around the park so that other members of the class can gather and record details. Pupils should also listen to the in-game radio broadcast, as this provides some simple persuasive language and models for some features of a typical radio advertisement. After around 15 minutes of exploration discuss, as a class, children's descriptions and add to the list that was created at the start of the lesson.

Explain to the pupils that they will now create a radio advertisement. Create success criteria for a 'great radio advert'.

Points to consider:

- powerful verbs/adjectives for effect: e.g. Climb aboard the ferocious, heart-stopping roller coaster...

- use of persuasive devices to engage the listener: e.g. Don't look like a baby in front of your friends. Show them you're the bravest! Try our new bumper cars...

- informal/conversational language: e.g. Isn't it time you and your mates had a wild day out?

- use of rhetorical questions: Bored? Tired of the same old days out? Always feeling like you never do anything exciting? Well, have we got a theme park for you!

- be concise! (Limit pupils to a 2-3 minute advert.)

- use of numbers/percentages: e.g. 95% of visitors claim this was the best day out they had ever had. Our roller coaster will make you feel amazing....

- use of present tense to describe the rides.

After establishing these expectations, pupils should begin to write their advertisements. Pupils should be encouraged to use any vocabulary collected on the 'working document' to help to create their advert. (Allow pupils approximately 25 minutes to create and rehearse their advertisements.)

When they are completed, pupils should share their adverts with the class. Teachers may wish to record the adverts. This can then form the basis of peer assessments...

e.g. It was really good when you used a rhetorical question...

Next time, to make it even better, try to add more descriptive words...

Pupils should be instructed to conduct peer-assessment positively, aiming for two or three positive comments to any one suggested improvement.

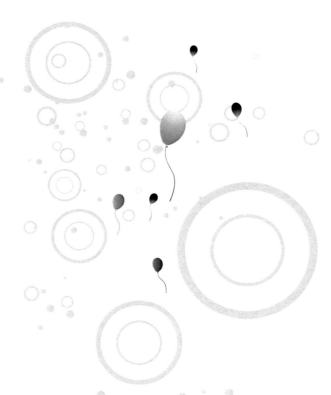

Activity Six: To write a diary entry based upon a day at a theme park

Target/s

To write a diary entry, including detailed descriptions of thoughts and feelings

How long?

60 minutes

Equipment

- Xbox 360 console (including Hard Disk Drive)

- *Thrillville: Off The Rails* Demo (needs to be downloaded before the lesson from the Xbox Live Marketplace)

- Projector

- Activity Sheet 6

Group size

Whole-class activity

Concept

In this activity, the exciting stimulus will help pupils to create an involved diary entry. Exploring the park and experiencing the rides will evoke feelings that are meaningful for the pupil, which in turn will assist pupils in their writing of a diary entry with a more engaged, realistic feel.

Game set-up

- Follow instructions for setting up the Xbox 360 as shown on page 2 - 4.

- Follow 'Game set-up' instructions as shown on pages 34 and 35.

Activity

Open the lesson by asking pupils about 'days out' that they have had. Briefly discuss some of the day trips that the pupils have been involved in; ask if they enjoyed their day out, and why. Tell the pupils that they are going to be experiencing a day out at a theme park using the games console.

Introduce the game to the pupils and allow them the opportunity to explore the theme park. All rides can be accessed by just walking up to them using the left directional stick and pressing A. When on a ride, the camera will take on a first-person view as the ride begins. The viewpoint can be changed by using the Y button. Teachers may wish to invite pupils to control the character for short periods of time thereby allowing many pupils to experience the game.

While exploring the theme park, pupils should make notes using the photocopiable Activity Six sheet (page 39). Model how to make brief notes on the 'note cards' on the sheet. Tell the pupils to leave the bottom 'card' until the theme park has been fully explored. After exploring the theme park, encourage pupils to make their own evaluative judgement of the park. This will help pupils to create a more personalised diary account in which they express a personal subjective opinion. Give them time to discuss their views with a friend.

Once the notes and discussion have been completed, explain that they are going to be writing a diary extract based upon a day at Throttleville theme park. Establish success criteria with the pupils (dependent on age/ability of the group):

- Use at least two thoughts and two feelings: 'I felt anxious before I went on the roller coaster, but after the ride I realised it wasn't that bad!'

- Write in the past tense: 'We went to... I explored...'

- Write in the first person: 'I...We...'

- Write expressively: 'I can't believe I had to go there! I mean, it was really, really boring!'

- Recount in chronological order: 'That morning we set off to Throttleville... Finally my time had come to go on the biggest ride in the park...'

- Write descriptively about the events that occurred: 'My heart was racing like a motor car as the cold sweat dripped down my forehead... my time had come to go on the ferocious-looking ride...'

Teachers may wish to model the opening paragraph of a diary entry linked to the success criteria. When diaries are completed, allow pupils time to self or peer-evaluate their writing

Extension

To extend this activity, teachers may wish to ask pairs of pupils to assume the roles of siblings who have just visited the park. Allocate the roles so that one sibling enjoys the day, and one does not. This will then create a diary of contrasting ideas and views based on the same shared experience.

What did you think of the theme park? Why?

Use the space on this page to make some notes about your visit to the theme park.

What ride did you like the least? Why?

What was your favourite ride? Why?

How would you describe the theme park? (Use all of your senses!)

Would you go back to the theme park again? Why?

Activity Seven: To write an explanation of a created theme-park ride

Target/s

To create a theme-park ride, considering style, type and appearance

To explain clearly how the ride works

How long?

2 hours (which can be extended/shortened based upon group size and/or time restrictions)

Equipment

- Xbox 360 console (including Hard Disk Drive)

- *Thrillville: Off The Rails* Demo (needs to be downloaded before the lesson from the Xbox Live Marketplace)

- Projector

- Access to computers

- Photographs of theme-park rides

- Drawing equipment

Group size

Grouped work (3-4 pupils per group)

Concept

The demo version of *Thrillville: Off The Rails* allows a 'taster' of ride creation. This experience provides a stimulus which helps pupils to create imaginative theme-park rides. Pupils can observe how the rides move and this will help them to explain their own ride. This activity also blends genres of writing, allowing for assessment of the pupils' understanding of both creative and non-fiction writing. This activity also integrates skills from other curriculum areas such as Art and ICT.

Game set-up

- Follow instructions for setting up the Xbox 360 as shown on pages 2 - 4.

- Follow 'Game set-up' instructions as shown on page 34 and 35.

Activity

As a class, watch the clip of the professor at the start of the game. This will give the pupils a context in which to work. Explore the park and allow pupils time to go on the rides. All rides can be accessed by just walking up to them using the left directional stick and pressing A. During a ride the camera will take on a first-person view as the ride begins. The viewpoint can be changed by using the Y button. Teachers may wish to invite pupils to come and control the character for short periods of time, thereby allowing many pupils to experience the game.

After exploring the theme park, encourage pupils to place their own rides. To do this:

- Follow the road (using the left directional stick). On the right-hand side of the park there is an open space. Walk into the open space. This will turn the circular icon in the bottom right-hand corner of the screen into a brick icon with a flashing A button.

- Press A to access the menu. Children will then be given the option to build either a carnival ride, game or stall. Move the left directional stick to the preferred option and press A.

- Move the left directional stick left or right to choose a ride.

- Select a ride/attraction by pressing A and then you will be asked where to place it. This can be done by moving the directional stick to position the ride and the right and left bumpers, RB and LB, to rotate the ride. The ride can be placed when it is shaded blue. If it is shaded red, there is not enough space for it.

- To place the ride, press A.

While pupils are choosing rides, they should be asked questions which help them to evaluate their choices:

- Why did you choose that ride?

- How does the ride move? Up and down? In a circuit? Around obstacles?

- Could the ride be placed anywhere else? Why/why not?

- Does the ride fit in with the others around it? Why?

- Do you think the ride will be popular? Why?

Group the pupils into threes or fours. At this stage the teacher may wish to assign roles in the group or allow pupils to choose their own roles within the group. Clearly explain to the pupils what they will be asked to produce:

- A brand new ride design (This will be drawn carefully, from a variety of views and labelled using detail about materials, colour etc.)

- An explanation of how it will work (This can be written down and then explained orally to the group.)

- They will need to present their work to the group. (This may involve the use of ICT, for example Microsoft Power Point or Photo Story 3.)

Children will then begin the task of creating a new ride. Pictures of theme-park rides could provide another useful visual stimulus for pupils at this stage. The teacher should ensure the quality of the design through further questioning:

- What do you want your ride to look like?

- Is the ride going to be designed to be scary? How will you achieve this?

- How many people will the ride hold at once?

- How tall/wide will the ride be?

- What will the ride be called? Does the name reflect what the ride does?

Once the pupils have finalised a design, allow time for them to create an accurate set of drawings. The teacher may wish to explain the need to add labels and captions to diagrams.

When the designs are completed, pupils should write a detailed explanation of how their ride works. Establish success criteria for their explanations:

- clear structure: introduction, explanation of parts of the ride, explanation of how it works, conclusion;

- present tense;

- a range of connectives (consequently, in addition...);

- use of specific details in writing (the steel locking mechanism...).

Once the success criteria have been discussed the pupils can begin to write explanations of how the ride works. Pupils should be encouraged to refer back to their designs and the success criteria in order to create a clear and concise explanation of their ride.

When the explanation has been completed, allow pupils a short rehearsal time before they present their work to the class. During the presentation, the teacher may wish to ask the groups questions, or allow the other pupils time to ask the presenters about their work. Refer to the success criteria when feeding back to the pupils after their presentations.

Activity Eight: To write a formal letter of complaint based upon a day at a theme park

Target

To create a formal piece of writing based upon an imaginary event

To write formally and consider a target audience

How long?

60 minutes

Equipment

- Xbox 360 console (including Hard Disk Drive)
- *Thrillville: Off The Rails* demo (needs to be downloaded before the lesson from the Xbox Live Marketplace)
- Projector
- Examples of different types of letters (letter of complaint, agony aunt, correspondence)

Group size

Whole-class activity

Concept

In this activity, pupils take a critical look at the theme park. Pupils are encouraged to use exploration time to identify negative aspects of the theme park. With their evidence gathered, pupils then write a letter to the 'professor' of the park stating their concerns. This can be further developed into a role-play activity.

Game set-up

- Follow instructions for setting up the Xbox 360 as shown on pages 2 - 4.
- Follow 'Game set-up' instructions as shown on pages 34 and 35.

Activity

Tell the pupils that they will be taking on the role of a theme-park critic. Establish what this means, and ensure that pupils understand that they are looking for negative points while exploring the park. Show pupils Activity Sheet 8 on page 45, and model how to use it by writing the essential nature of the problem in the small box and then adding more detail in the large box below.

Allow pupils time to explore the theme park, reminding them that they are looking for negative features:

- Are there any safety issues within the park?
- Is it well designed for different groups of visitor? (older people, young people, people with disabilities?)
- Are there enough amenities in the park? (food, toilets etc.)

Establish with the pupils that they are aiming to outline three different areas of concern (this number can be differentiated to suit the group). Allow enough time for pupils to gather negative aspects of the park and encourage them to add extra details in the larger boxes on the activity sheet.

Explain to the pupils that they are now going to write a critical letter to the professor using the information they have just researched. Discuss what type of letter this should be; formal or informal? Clarify the differences and, as a class, conclude that a formal letter is more appropriate in this situation. At this point it would be useful for pupils to see examples of formal letters/ formal vocabulary in order to aid this task.

Create success criteria for the letter:

- must be in a formal style;

- clear paragraphs explaining the range of issues identified in their park visit;

- clear opening and closing of the letter;

- correct layout of a letter;

- use of higher-level connectives (e.g. however, furthermore, in addition, therefore).

Pupils then proceed to write their letters, using the activity sheet and referring to the success criteria throughout.

When the letter-writing is completed, allow pupils time to self - or peer - evaluate their work, based upon the success criteria chosen for the task.

Extension

Invite a pupil to take on the role of 'the professor' of the park. During this hot-seating session, the other pupils ask 'the professor' questions, based on what they discovered during their evaluation of the park e.g.

'What will you do about the lack of toilets in the theme park?'

The pupil taking on the role of professor needs to think about how to address the issue and, where possible, should offer a solution to the problem. The professor can be played by a number of pupils during the activity.

For a further extension activity, photocopy the pupils' letters and hand them out to different pupils in the class. Explain that the pupils are now going to become 'the professor', and write a reply to the critic, explaining what they intend to do about their concerns.

Activity Eight:
To write a formal letter of complaint about a theme park

Tuesday 30th March.

L.O. To use persuasive language to describe a theme park.

COME TO
Throttleville !!!

Tierd of any old, boring theme park? Why not come to Throttleville the UK's leading best themepark for 2010? Where you and your family can come, ~~from 8am till late~~.

If you come either this ~~next~~ week or next you ~~may get~~ are guarenteed to get a discount 50% off all rides. We have a selection of ~~feet~~ breath-taking rides. Feel the laughter as you challenge your friends and family.

~~en~~ Enjoy racing 100mph down our fast ~~is~~ however but friendly Rollacoaster as the wind blows your hair back. Every rides is checked daily by our eco-friendly staff.

I felt confident with my work

We are open at:
(Mon - Thu) 8.00am - 8pm
Fri = 9.00am - 7pm
Sat = 8am - 9.30pm
Sun = 9.30am - 3pm
Just off the M6.

SO WHY NOT COME !!!

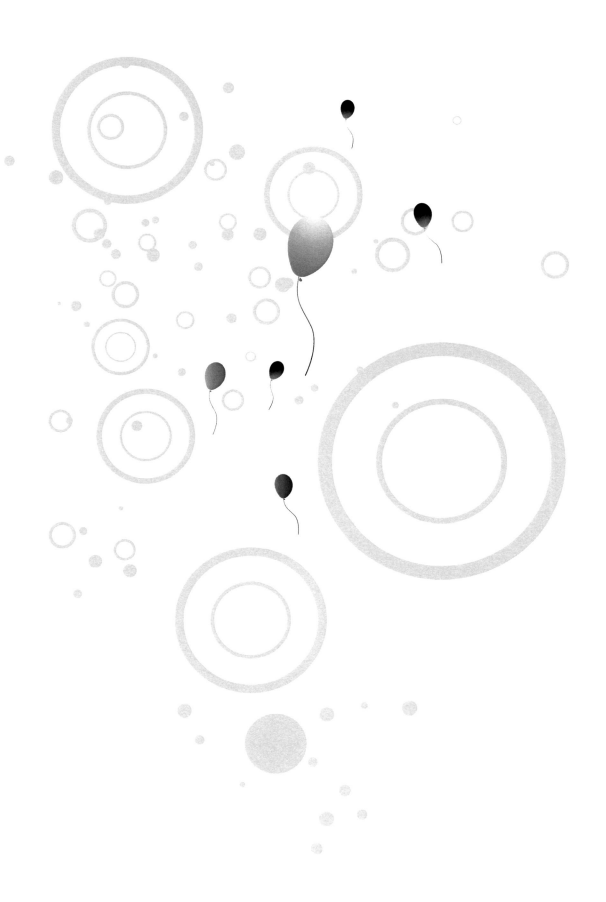

PUPIL EXAMPLE: THRILLVILLE

12+
Please note, this game has been rated 12+

Synopsis

Kameo is an action/adventure game created by Rare. Players assume the role of Kameo, the princess of an elf kingdom, who is able to transform into a variety of powerful alter egos. These diverse abilities help Kameo to overcome the numerous trials she faces throughout her quest. The game's graphics are visually stunning and the game's fantasy setting is highly detailed and full of interesting sights and sounds.

There are two versions of the game demo. The New Kameo Demo is the one that will be used for the activities in this section. The demo has four distinct sections which have varied time limits:

✴ Fight in a massive battle (1 minute)*
✴ Explore a fantasy world (4 minutes)
✴ Invade a crumbling castle (3 minutes)*
✴ Destroy a huge monster(6 minutes)*

The time limits help to ensure that the lesson is pacey.

The activities in this section will all be creative-writing focused and can be used together as an effective whole topic or as individual activities.

*Contains fantasy violence

Controls in Game
Full controls can be seen when a section has been chosen to play.

Basic Controls

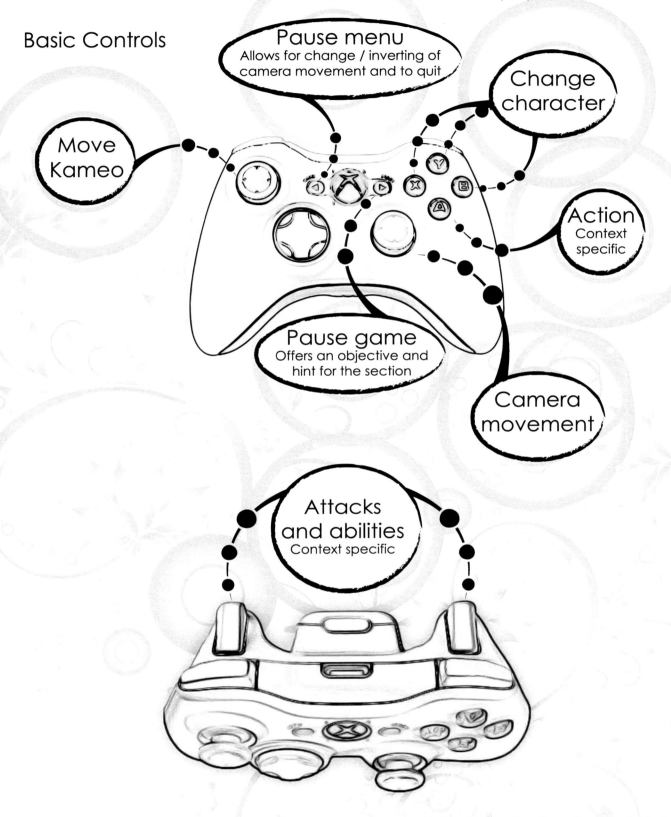

Pause menu
Allows for change / inverting of
camera movement and to quit

Change
character

Move
Kameo

Action
Context
specific

Pause game
Offers an objective and
hint for the section

Camera
movement

Attacks
and abilities
Context specific

Controls are not too challenging. However, manipulation of both directional sticks is useful with this game. The demo may return to the opening screen following a period of inaction (e.g. 30 seconds without moving the character).

Activity Nine: To explore who Kameo is

Target/s

✷ To use description (visual and auditory) of a character to ascertain identity

✷ To use deduction to identify a character

✷ To take on the role of, and empathise with, a character from a fantasy setting

How long?

The relevant section of the demo has a 4-minute time limit, but can be replayed as many times as required.

Activity 45-60 minutes

Equipment

✷ Xbox 360 console (including Hard Disk Drive)

✷ New Kameo Demo (needs to be downloaded before the lesson from the Xbox Live Marketplace)

✷ Projector

✷ Images of Kameo http://www.rare.co.uk/games/kameo-elements-of-power

Group size

Whole-class activity

Concept

Exploring the richly detailed environment of the game will allow children to build up an understanding of who Kameo is. Owing to the excellent visual and audio effects used in the game, pupils will be sufficiently engaged to describe the character of Kameo in a detailed and convincing way. This will allow pupils to develop multi-sensory descriptions, as an aid to future writing. By interacting with the in-game characters, pupils will be able to deduce who Kameo is conversationally, adding depth to the character and dynamically illustrating to pupils how to describe characters in a variety of ways. Hot-seating will encourage empathic response thereby allowing for more emotional and thoughtful character development in writing.

Game set-up

✷ Follow instructions for setting up the Xbox 360 as shown on page 2.

✷ Turn the Xbox 360 on.

✷ Under 'My Xbox' scroll right to 'Games Library' using the left directional stick.

✷ Press A. (The game demos should appear on the 'Recent Games' list.)

✷ Scroll down using the left directional stick to the Kameo demo.

✷ Press Y with the demo selected and it will load automatically.

✳ Press *Start* when prompted.

✳ The screen will now read 'I want to...' and give four choices.

✳ **For this activity choose: '...explore a fantasy kingdom'.** Press A to accept.

✳ During the loading screen the controls will be shown.

✳ Press A when directed to begin the demo.

Activity

Show an image of the main character, Kameo. (Use the above link for a screenshot of her.) In pairs ask pupils to orally describe her. Note descriptions and praise thoughtful and developed description.

Ask pupils:

'Do these descriptions tell us everything about Kameo?'

Discuss this until the class has reasonably concluded that more information is needed about Kameo before she can be described accurately. As a class, explore what needs to be discovered about her in order to describe the character fully. This might include aspects such as:

✳ how she moves;

✳ how other people react to her in the kingdom;

✳ any background information about her.

Explain to the pupils that they are now going to take control of Kameo and explore the Kingdom in which she lives. Ask for a volunteer to control Kameo. Use the map on page 51 to aid exploration.

During this time encourage the pupil in control of Kameo to talk to as many of the villagers as possible and read and listen carefully to what they have to say. While there are some characters with only a small amount to say, there are others who will provide clues as to who Kameo is. Key characters have a bubble marked '...' above their heads. These 'key information' characters have their approximate locations shown on the map.

As the area is being explored, encourage pupils to add notes to the Activity Nine sheet, 'Who is Kameo?'. Teachers may wish to model how to make notes on the sheet prior to pupil writing.

When clues are given in conversation about who Kameo is, discuss these with the pupils and allow them to deduce who Kameo is from the conversations seen and heard.

The demo will automatically end after four minutes and the next part of the demo will begin. In order to remain focussed on this section, when the timer is almost over: press Back button on the remote then move the left directional stick down to quit and press A, then press A again. This will bring the demo back to the starting screen, allowing the activity to be repeated as many times as needed.

When the kingdom has been explored, encourage pupils to discuss who they think Kameo is, based on what they have seen/heard.

Invite a pupil to take on the role of Kameo in hot-seating. This will allow children to develop an understanding of the type of thoughts and feelings she may have, and to create an empathy with a character in a fantasy setting.

Encourage other pupils to ask questions. Encourage the use of open questioning to elicit responses that require thoughts and feelings.

These could include:

✳ 'How did you feel when you found out your family had been kidnapped?'

✳ 'What is it like to have such a huge castle for a home?'

✳ 'What will you do about your family being missing?'

Once a number of pupils have had the opportunity to take on the hot-seat role of Kameo, establish the character of Kameo as a class and create a character profile of her.

Activity Nine:
Map of the Enchanted Kingdom

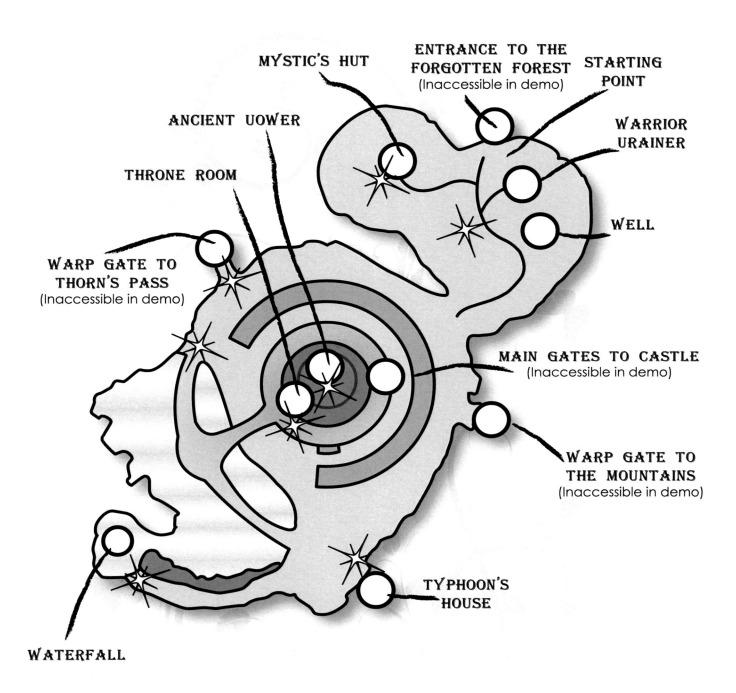

MYSTIC'S HUT

ENTRANCE TO THE
FORGOTTEN FOREST
(Inaccessible in demo)

STARTING
POINT

ANCIENT UOWER

WARRIOR
URAINER

THRONE ROOM

WELL

WARP GATE TO
THORN'S PASS
(Inaccessible in demo)

MAIN GATES TO CASTLE
(Inaccessible in demo)

WARP GATE TO
THE MOUNTAINS
(Inaccessible in demo)

TYPHOON'S
HOUSE

WATERFALL

Is the approximate location of a key character with
information regarding Kameo and her background. These are only
approximates as the characters will move and behave like real people.

Activity Nine:
Who is Kameo?

As you explore the kingdom, write down your thoughts in the boxes below.

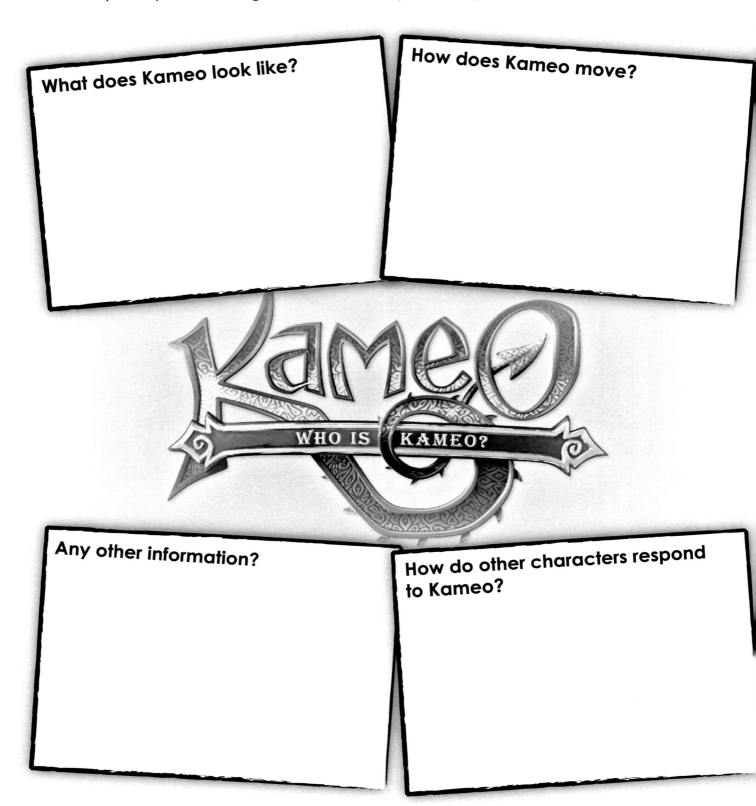

What does Kameo look like?

How does Kameo move?

Any other information?

How do other characters respond to Kameo?

Activity Ten: To describe a fantasy setting focusing on multi-sensory and positional language

Target/s

To produce a multi-sensory description of a fantasy setting which includes positional language

How long?

The section has a 4-minute time limit but can be replayed as many times as required.

Activity 45-60 minutes

Equipment

✳ Xbox 360 console (including Hard Disk Drive)

✳ New Kameo Demo (needs to be downloaded before the lesson from the Xbox Live Marketplace)

✳ Projector

Group size

Whole-class activity (paired work in some areas)

Concept

The kingdom of the game provides pupils with a vivid location to explore and describe. This location also contains many of the features of a fantasy setting that pupils may already be aware of. This activity will allow pupils to develop their understanding of this type of setting in a particularly immersive way. In addition to the excellent location, the game adopts a day/night cycle which can be experienced during the four minutes. This is another great feature which pupils can then draw upon in their own descriptive writing.

Game set-up

✳ Follow instructions for setting up the Xbox 360 as shown on pages 2 and 3.

✳ Follow 'Game set-up' instructions as shown on pages 48 and 49 until the screen reads 'I want to...' and gives four choices.

✳ **For this activity choose: '...explore a fantasy kingdom'.** Press A to accept.

✳ During the loading screen the controls will be shown.

✳ Press A when directed to begin the demo.

Activity

Ask the pupils what they understand by a 'fantasy setting'. Gather examples and keep them as a 'working document' throughout the activity. While pupils explore the kingdom, the teacher/pupils may wish to add additional features to the list to aid future writing.

Explain to the pupils that during this lesson they are going to explore a fantasy kingdom and that during this time the pupils will need to look out for interesting things within the kingdom.

A map to help with movement can be found on page 56.

On the first viewing, explore only the outside locations. Invite one pupil to take control of Kameo and encourage the other pupils to work in pairs (using the photocopiable sheet for Activity Ten), writing anything they would use to describe this location, and the positions of the points of interest (e.g. the castle is high above the town).

This could be turned into a game by giving prizes (house points etc.) to the winning group. This will encourage detailed descriptions of the digital environment.

As a class, discuss what was seen and, if needed, add new suggestions to the fantasy-setting 'working document'.

Discuss with the class how to describe a setting effectively. Establishing multi-sensory description is imperative:

✶ What can we see?

✶ What can we hear?

✶ What could we touch?

✶ What could we smell?

✶ What could we taste?

✶ How might we describe the position of objects?

Invite pupils to create sentences based on what they have already spotted during the exploration. Share examples of the sentences as a class and highlight effective examples.

On the second tour, focus on internal locations. Encourage the use of all senses to describe the inside of the buildings around the kingdom. Many of the small huts have very similar interiors so, in order to work within the time limit, aim to look inside one hut before moving on to the castle.

During the third tour of the environment, invite other pupils to instruct the pupil in control so that any areas the class still wish to explore can be seen. In addition to moving around the kingdom, make special note of the change between day and night:

✶ What differences can be seen?

✶ What differences can be heard?

When all exploration has been completed, compile a list of powerful words and phrases that could be used to describe the kingdom. Encourage pupils to use these notes and focus on using the senses to develop engaging locational writing.

Create success criteria for writing the descriptive paragraph. Focus on:

- ✳ use of all senses;

- ✳ a variety of powerful adjectives and adverbs;

- ✳ clear use of positional language;

- ✳ use of both simile and metaphor for description;

- ✳ a variety of sentence types and constructions.

Give pupils the time to write a paragraph describing the Enchanted Kingdom setting. Encourage the pupils to use their notes and focus on the success criteria to write a detailed description of the setting.

Once the activity is completed, allow pupils time to self - or peer - assess their work based upon the success criteria.

Activity Ten:
Map of the Enchanted Kingdom

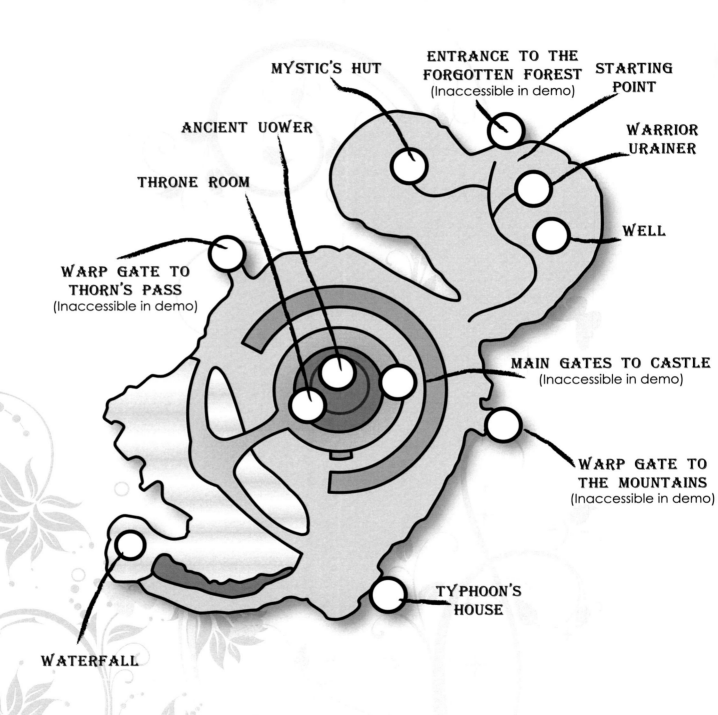

MYSTIC'S HUT

ENTRANCE TO THE
FORGOTTEN FOREST
(Inaccessible in demo)

STARTING
POINT

ANCIENT UOWER

WARRIOR
URAINER

THRONE ROOM

WELL

WARP GATE TO
THORN'S PASS
(Inaccessible in demo)

MAIN GATES TO CASTLE
(Inaccessible in demo)

WARP GATE TO
THE MOUNTAINS
(Inaccessible in demo)

TYPHOON'S
HOUSE

WATERFALL

Activity Ten: To describe a fantasy setting using the senses

What could you: **S**ee   **H**ear   **S**mell   **T**ouch   **T**aste

The outside environment of the Kingdom	The buildings in the Kingdom	Day	Night

Activity Eleven: To create a fantasy-style character based upon the Elemental Warriors

Target

To develop a unique character considering both appearance and abilities

How long?

The section has a 6-minute time limit but can be replayed as many times as required.

Activity 60 minutes

Equipment

* Xbox 360 console (including Hard Disk Drive)

* New Kameo Demo (needs to be downloaded before the lesson from the Xbox Live Marketplace)

* Projector

* Word processor (optional)

Group size

Whole-class activity (paired work in some areas)

Concept

The key to Kameo's success in the game is utilising the power of the Elemental Warriors, into which she can transform. This helps her to defeat her enemies and complete tasks during her quest. Using the game as an example, pupils can develop their own Elemental Warrior; thinking about what it will look like, how it will behave and also how it will benefit Kameo. The game provides pupils with an engaging, imaginative scenario.

Game set-up

* Follow instructions for setting up the Xbox 360 as shown on pages 2 and 3.

* Follow 'Game set-up' instructions as shown on pages 48 and 49 until the screen reads 'I want to...' and gives four choices.

* **For this activity choose: '...invade a crumbling castle'.** Press A to accept.
(It will not be needed straight away. See below for when it is required.)

* During the loading screen the controls will be shown.

* Press A when directed to begin the demo.

Activity

Leave the game idle for a short period of time and a short video sequence will play which shows Kameo changing into many forms (Elemental Warriors). Discuss why they might be called Elemental Warriors and discuss the elements that can be seen (e.g. fire, ice). Explain to the pupils that these are special powers that Kameo can control and use to help her in her adventure.

Press start and move the left directional stick down to '...invade a crumbling castle' and press A. This section of the demo allows Kameo to change into three distinct Elemental Warriors:

✳ Chilla (Ice) - Press X to activate. Yeti-type creature

✳ Pummel Weed (Plant) - Press Y to activate. Venus flytrap-type creature

✳ Major Ruin (Rock) - Press B to activate. Armadillo-type creature

The distinctive moves that each Elemental Warrior can perform are shown on screen when they are chosen.

Allow pupils time to experiment with each of Kameo's incarnations. While this is happening, encourage the other members of the class to consider the following questions about the characters:

✳ How do they look?

✳ How do they move?

✳ What element do they represent?

✳ What skills/attacks do they have?

Discuss the individual Elemental Warriors as a class. Ask pupils to make evaluative comments based on what they have seen...

'Which Elemental Warrior do you think is the strongest? Why?'

'Which Elemental Warrior do you think will be the most useful? Why?'

Explain to the pupils that they are going to create their own Elemental Warrior and a web page with information about it. The pupils will need to decide which element to choose. It may be necessary to create a list of elements, as a class, to assist with this choice.

Once the element has been chosen, pupils should create a diagram of their creature. They should consider its movement, skills and attacks. Establish that this is a report text with descriptive language and create success criteria based upon the task (this will vary depending on group and age of pupils):

✳ present tense;

✳ descriptive, factual language;

✳ similar information grouped in paragraphs (e.g. description, basic techniques, advanced techniques);

✳ when the task is complete, pupils can self-assess against the success criteria.

Extension

Using a word processor, the Elemental Warrior's description can be turned into a web page. In addition, it would be straightforward to then email pupils' work to Rare, providing pupils with real life relevance for the task (editor@rare.co.uk).

Activity Twelve: To write a fantasy story using Kameo

Target

To write a fantasy narrative based on the Kameo: elements of power world

How long?

The different sections of the demo have different time limits (up to six minutes per section)

60 minutes +

Equipment

* Xbox 360 console (including Hard Disk Drive)
* New Kameo Demo (needs to be downloaded before the lesson from the Xbox Live Marketplace)
* Projector

Group size

Whole-class activity (paired work in some areas)

Concept

As the demo is divided into different sections, a narrative can be created which varies location and situation. Each has dynamic music and engaging camera work. All of these stimuli will encourage children to write and describe in a far more detailed and exciting way.

Game set-up

* Follow instructions for setting up the Xbox 360 as shown on pages 2 and 3.
* Follow 'Game set-up' instructions as shown on pages 48 and 49 until the screen reads 'I want to...' and gives four choices.
* **For this activity, this choice depends on which part of the activity you are performing.**
* During the loading screen the controls will be shown.
* Press A when directed to begin the demo.

Activity

Explain to the pupils that they will be writing a narrative in the fantasy genre, using the game to help to develop an interesting plot. Establish success criteria for writing a story in a fantasy setting (which will vary depending on group/age).

- ✴ use of action, description and dialogue to describe a character;

- ✴ powerful adjectives and adverbs to describe settings ;

- ✴ use of a clear structure (paragraphs);

- ✴ description of both the thoughts and feelings of the character;

- ✴ gripping description of action/events;

- ✴ buildup of tension using a variety of different sentence types (e.g. short sentences).

Here is a breakdown of teaching points for each element of the story structure:

Question words	Demo section needed	Information for teaching
Who?	'...to explore a fantasy world'	Kameo is clearly seen, the camera can pan around her showing her in detail. (Activity One in this section looks at her character in detail.)
Where?	'...to explore a fantasy world'	The Enchanted Kingdom can be fully explored and has a variety of interior and exterior environments and also runs on a day/night cycle. (Activity Two in this section looks in detail at the setting.)
Where next?	'...to fight in a massive battle'	This section allows the player a minute to explore a huge battle on horseback. This can be linked into the journey to the Forgotten Forest.
Why?		This is explained by The Mystic in the Enchanted Kingdom (Kameo's Uncle Halis is being held captive in the Forgotten Forest). Can be developed by pupils.
What goes wrong?	'...destroy a huge monster'	Old Mawood, The monster is holding Halis captive inside him.
Who helps?		Kameo is alone, but uses her powers to help her. (Activity Three develops the ideas of powers and pupils may have previously created their own 'elemental warrior' powers.)
Where last?	'...to explore a fantasy world'	Would be imagined, with her uncle freed.
Feelings?		Developed by the pupils.

Use the table and work through each section. As a group, tell the story of what is happening aloud, with the teacher leading. The activity sheet on page 64 will allow the children to make notes as the story is being told so that they can plan their narrative carefully.

It would be beneficial for a teacher or other member of staff to control Kameo through these sections thereby allowing children to concentrate on the task. The controls are very simple. I would recommend not performing any of the actions suggested on screen in each section of the demo.

Load the demo and choose '...explore a fantasy world'.

Below is an example of how the story could be expressed orally:

Kameo stared out into the Enchanted Kingdom on a warm spring morning. She had heard that a local mystic had news for her. Her jet black hair glistened in the sun as she searched for him. (Check map for location of the Mystic's house.) *Kameo sensed that something was wrong that day, yet she could not guess what manner of tragic news she was about to hear.* (Speak to the Mystic by pressing A. He tells Kameo about the kidnapping of her uncle.)

Anxious, distressed and frightened, Kameo knew in her mind that she must try and save her uncle. I'm the only one who can do this, she thought, as she prepared for the journey. (Leave the section by pressing 'back' and quitting by pressing A and A to confirm. Then press A on '...fight in a massive battle'.) *Kameo climbed upon her brave horse and prepared to face the hordes of evil Trolls to find a route to the Forgotten Forest. The howls and screams of hundreds of battle-thirsty Trolls pierced the air. Kameo took in one last deep, lingering breath before riding down the hill face.* (Move Kameo down the hill on horseback using the left directional stick.) *Trolls clambered to reach her yet her speed and determination brought her through. Behind her she heard the battle cry of the Kingdom's soldiers as they raced to fend off the evil force that was trying to invade her kingdom.* (This section of the demo only lasts one minute. When the time is up, quit as before and stop the game briefly.)

At this point discuss why Kameo is going to go to the Forgotten Forest. Hot-seating would be excellent in order to ascertain the thoughts and feelings of the main character. As the Forgotten Forest is not featured in the demo, it will be up to the pupils to create the location. This will allow children to be creative in designing their own setting.

When this section has been written, begin the demo again, selecting '...fight a huge monster' option. The demo will begin again with Kameo in combat.

Racing through the tall temple doors, Kameo quickly realised that to free her Uncle would take all her strength. The monstrous enemy she faced stood towering menacingly above her.

At this point allow the pupils to describe the character themselves, discussing the best suggestions as a group. To show the attacks that the enemy possesses it will be necessary to keep moving around the outside of the enemy: this will illustrate what manner of threat Kameo is under. Then pause the demo and ask the children to think about how Kameo could defeat the enemy. Allow time for discussion, then writing of ideas. Quit the demo as before then re-select '...explore a fantasy world'.

With Uncle Halis back safely in the Kingdom, Kameo felt a sense of relief and happiness. She had had the strength to save him. She stared out into the water of the lake and knew that this was only the beginning of her long journey, that there would be many other dangers to face in the future. She smiled as a squirrel raced along the pathway. "I will do it," she said to herself, before making her way up to the castle. Nightfall began to set in. (End the demo by quitting as before.)

The story told will vary greatly with different groups and ages.

Allow time for the children to complete their own narrative and self - or peer - assess their story against the success criteria.

Extension

It may be possible for the children to edit and redraft their story on to a word processor and/or the story could be recorded orally and used in other classes.

Activity Twelve:
To write a story in a fantasy setting

Story Planning Sheet

Who?	
Where?	
Where next?	
Why?	
What goes wrong?	
Who helps?	
Where last?	
Feelings?	

Synopsis

Viva Piñata: Trouble In Paradise is the second game in the series by developer Rare. Players assume the role of maintainers of plots of land on Piñata Island. On their plot the player must entice, maintain and breed a wide variety of various 'piñatas'. The piñata are based upon well-known animals (e.g. hedgehogs) but in the game they have amusing names based upon well-known sweets (e.g. Fudgehog).

The demo gives a 25-minute taster of the main game. The player is asked to complete a small tutorial each time the game loads. However this can be ignored and for the purposes of the following activities it should be (unless otherwise stated).

The game controls can be simplified and in many cases should be for younger children. The controls for both types are shown below. To choose simple controls press **start** while in the game and choose the option for simple controls.

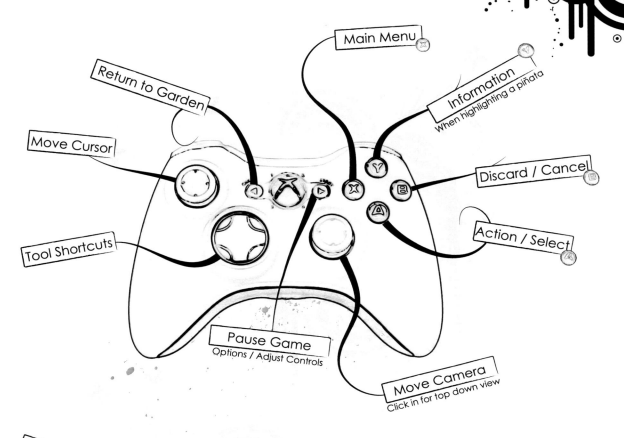

Main Menu

Information
When highlighting a piñata

Return to Garden

Move Cursor

Discard / Cancel

Tool Shortcuts

Action / Select

Pause Game
Options / Adjust Controls

Move Camera
Click in for top down view

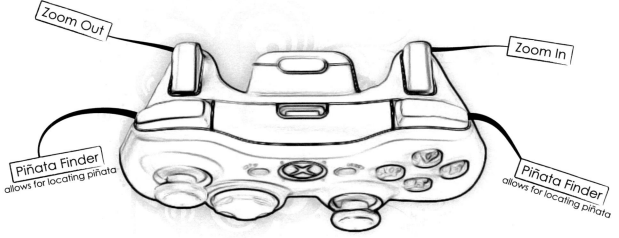

Zoom Out

Zoom In

Piñata Finder
allows for locating piñata

Piñata Finder
allows for locating piñata

Simple Controls

This control scheme just uses the left directional stick (left/right moves around the cursor, up/down moves the player forwards/backwards). The A,B,Y&X buttons all do the same regardless of controls chosen. (Controls are set at *simple* by default.)

Piñata name list

These are the piñata that are already in the garden at the start of the demo, and also those piñata that *may* visit the garden as the game progresses.

Custacean

Pretztail

Pengum

Lemmoning

Bispotti

Whirlm

Mothdrop

Walrusk

Arocknid

Sparrowmint

(Owing to the nature of the game, other piñata may visit the garden!)

An interesting opener to the following set of activities would be to give out the above names and ask pupils to work out which animal and which confectionery the animal's name is created from (e.g. Walrusk is walrus and rusk).

Activity Thirteen: To create a report based upon an imagined piñata

Target

To write a report based upon a created animal, using Viva Piñata as a stimulus

How long?

The demo has a 25-minute approximate time limit but can be replayed as many times as required. Activity: 120 minutes

Equipment

✹ Xbox 360 console (including Hard Disk Drive)

✹ Viva Piñata: Trouble In Paradise Demo (needs to be downloaded before the lesson from the Xbox Live Marketplace. See page 7.)

✹ Projector

Group size

Whole-class activity

Concept

The world of Viva Piñata is vibrant and colourful and designed with children in mind. The animals behave in many similar ways to their real-life counterparts, yet are sufficiently different to provide exciting variations from real life. This allows pupils to be creative with their imagined animal, and will lead to important use of non-fiction, descriptive writing (in a fictional setting), thereby improving both aspects of the pupil's writing. This lesson provides dynamic stimulus for report writing (at the end of a unit of work), or as a one-off text-revision lesson.

Game set-up

✹ Follow instructions for setting up the Xbox 360 as shown on pages 2 and 3.

✹ Turn the Xbox 360 on.

✹ Under 'My Xbox' scroll right to 'Games Library' using the left directional stick.

✹ Press A. (The game demos should appear on the Recent Games list.)

✹ Scroll down using the left directional stick to the FIFA 10 demo.

✹ Press Y with the demo selected and it will load automatically.

✹ Press *Start* when prompted.

✹ Press A on *Play a Garden*.

✹ Select *New Garden* with A.

✹ The demo will now load. There is an introductory film clip which can be skipped by pressing Start.

✹ Press *back* to access the garden when the Leafos introduction appears.

(IMPORTANT NOTE: The game will continue dynamically as the demo progresses; new piñata will visit the garden, some piñata may even fight with each other. It is not necessary to get involved in any of these events and all speech from characters can be skipped by pressing *Back*.)

Activity

Ask pupils to name some animals they know. Make a list of them, and discuss the features of a number of them. Discuss the key features of each animal (e.g. the size, colour, habitat). Explain to the pupils that they are going to explore a special type of area where piñatas live. Ensure that pupils do understand what is meant by a piñata before continuing.

Start the demo and invite a pupil to control the game and explore the garden. While doing this, encourage other pupils to make a list of all animals they recognise. When the list is created, consider each creature individually by placing the cursor over it. This will bring up the name of the creature and how happy/sad it is. Press the **Y** button to access information about the piñata, then press **Y** again to access the encyclopedia entry for the piñata.

The encyclopedia section is split into:

✱ information (a short paragraph giving background information about the piñata)

✱ Appear requirements (What the player needs to do/have in their garden to make piñata appear around the outside of their garden.)

✱ Visit requirements (What the player needs to do/have in their garden to make the piñata come into the garden.)

✱ Resident requirements (What the player needs to do/have in their garden to make a piñata become a resident in the garden.)

✱ Romance requirements (What the player needs to do/have in their garden to make the piñata breed in the garden.)

Romance is dealt with sensitively [if not scientifically accurately] in the game. The two piñatas do a 'romance dance', which in turn leads to an egg appearing and a baby piñata being born!

Depending on the age of the pupils, the teacher may wish to discuss the names of the piñata and the pun that has been created.

The sections provide pupils with a paragraph structure to use in their writing. It will be necessary to watch the piñata move, as well as to look at the homes in the game. (The 'in game' homes of the piñatas can even be viewed internally by pressing A while the habitat is highlighted.)

Look at a range of piñata, then encourage the pupils to talk about the distinctive features of each one.

When this activity is completed, focus on one particular piñata. Model how to plan a report about a piñata using the resource sheet on page 72. It is important to discuss how the plan needs to be slightly different from the game, in as much that appearance requirements will need to be reported instead of given as a set of instructions.

When this plan is modelled, success criteria need to be created and agreed as a class:

- simple structure (title, introduction, paragraphs about the piñata, concluding statement)

- use of generalised statements (Many experts believe that...)

- use of specific and technical vocabulary

- impersonal language

- use of considered adjectives/adverbs for accurate description

- high level connectives (consequently, in addition)

The teacher may wish to model how to open a report for a selected piñata.

Explain to the pupils that they are going to create a page of the piñata encyclopedia for a brand-new creature that they have just discovered. Allow pupils time to discuss what kind of piñata they wish to create and think about the key information they will need to share with the reader. Give the pupils the planning sheet (P72) and allow sufficient time for planning. Teachers may wish to give pupils the opportunity to draw their piñata while planning, in order to help them to visualise their creation.

Pupils will then need to write a report for their own piñata using the planning sheet and success criteria to guide them. Encourage pupils to refer to the success criteria throughout the activity. When completed, give pupils the opportunity to self-assess their work or allow time for peer-assessment. The teacher may wish to create an encyclopedia of the pupils' work to add to the class library.

Activity Thirteen: To create a report based upon an imagined piñata

Name
Basic information about the piñata
Piñata appearance information
Piñata visit information
Piñata resident information
Piñata romance information
Any other information

Activity Fourteen: To create a set of instructions for looking after a piñata

Target
To create clear instructions for looking after a piñata

How long?

The demo has a 25-minute (approximate) time limit but can be replayed as many times as required.

Activity: 45-60 minutes

Equipment

✹ Xbox 360 console (including Hard Disk Drive)

✹ Viva Piñata: Trouble In Paradise Demo (needs to be downloaded before the lesson from the Xbox Live Marketplace. See page 7)

✹ Projector

Group size

Whole-class activity

Concept

This lesson gives pupils the opportunity to create a set of instructions applicable to an 'in-game' situation, providing an interesting variation on instructions for an everyday activity. This activity can follow the previous activity (where pupils create their own piñata) or can function as a stand-alone activity. The lesson can be used to teach instructional writing, or may be used as an assessment activity at the end of unit of work on instructional writing.

Game set-up

✹ Follow instructions for setting up the Xbox 360 as shown on pages 2 and 3.

✹ Turn the Xbox 360 on.

✹ Under 'My Xbox' scroll right to 'Games Library' using the left directional stick.

✹ Press A. (The game demos should appear on the 'Recent Games' list.)

✹ Scroll down using the left directional stick to the FIFA 10 demo.

✹ Press Y with the demo selected and it will load automatically.

✹ Press *Start* when prompted.

✹ Press A on *play a garden*.

✹ Select *New Garden* with A.

✹ The demo will now load. There is an introductory film clip which can be skipped by pressing *Start*.

✹ Press *Back* to access the garden when the Leafos introduction appears.

(IMPORTANT NOTE: The game will continue dynamically as the demo progresses; new piñata will visit the garden, some piñata may even fight with each other. It is not necessary to get involved in any of these events and all speech from characters can be skipped by pressing 'Back'.)

Activity

Explain to the pupils that they will be creating a set of instructions for looking after a piñata (or their own piñata if Activity Thirteen has been completed). Establish the structure and language features of instructional writing and look at examples based on real-life contexts (e.g. hamster/rabbit care etc).

Set up the game demo and follow the instructions given, focusing on the language used:

'Press START'

'Press the Menu X button'

'Select the Village option'

Are the instructions easy to use? Why? Discuss the use of simple language / use of imperative verbs to open the instruction / short sentences etc.

When the characters pop up on screen with information, look at the instructions given. Encourage children to be critical of the layout of the instructions. (The fact that they are written in a long paragraph does not make them easy to read.) Use one of the examples (*Willy the Builder* is a good one) and as a class rewrite the instructions in a more user-friendly way:

Instructions for using *Willy the Builder*

✻ Return to the game by pressing A.

✻ Press X to open the menu.

✻ Select the *village* option.

✻ Open the store by selecting the icon that looks like Willy's head.

Does this clarify the instructions? Discuss why and display this model for pupils to refer to during their writing. Establish success criteria for the writing. (This can be adapted to suit age/ability):

✻ Use clear vocabulary.

✻ Use imperative verbs (Press, Hold, Move).

✻ Use bullet points or numbered points to help clarify instructions.

✻ Title should begin with 'How to...' (How to look after a Fudgehog piñata).

✻ Use clear chronological order.

✻ Use time connectives (firstly, next, after that).

✻ Use present tense.

✻ Use 2nd person e.g. "Jonathan looked up...".

Now focus on one piñata from the garden. Ask the pupils to imagine they are creating a set of instructions for a leaflet on how to look after the chosen piñata. Observe the piñata for a while, whilst encouraging pupils to discuss with a partner (or as a group) important instructions that could be written in order to look after that piñata:

'Build an igloo to house the Pengum.'

'Feed the Pengum a chilli seed to keep him warm.'

The instructions can be completely fictional, but the teacher may wish to use the encyclopedia function of the game. This can be done by moving the left directional stick over the desired piñata and pressing Y to access the information, then Y again to access the encyclopedia.

At this point, if the previous activity has been completed, the teacher may encourage pupils to take the previously created piñata and write a set of instructions for looking after it. If this lesson is to be a stand-alone lesson, the teacher may wish to choose a different piñata and allow pupils to create a set of instructions based on it. Encourage pupils to use the previously written sets of instructions and the success criteria as a guide.

When the writing is completed, ask the pupils to swap their instructions with a partner and peer-assess the instructions using the success criteria.

Extension
Pupils may be asked to turn the instructions into a leaflet, thus providing an opportunity for the addition of illustrations, captions and labels.

Activity Fifteen: To write a persuasive letter based upon the Viva Piñata world

Target/s

To write a letter persuading the villain of the game to stop hunting and hurting piñata

How long?

The demo has a 25-minute (approximate) time limit but can be replayed as many times as required.

Activity: 45-60 minutes

Equipment

* Xbox 360 console (including Hard Disk Drive)

* Viva Piñata: Trouble In Paradise Demo (needs to be downloaded before the lesson from the Xbox Live Marketplace. See page 7)

* Projector

Group size

Whole-class activity

Concept

The idea for this activity centres on the opening cinematic of the game. This video clip introduces the player to the villain of the game, Professor Pester. During the clip we learn that the Professor wants to hunt piñata and prevent them from being sent to the 'cannonata' (a large 'in-game' cannon that sends piñata to children around the world). By giving the letter a context such as this, pupils will immediately be drawn into the role of wanting to help the piñatas, a feeling that is even deeper if this activity follows the previous two activities in this section.

Game set-up

Follow the game set-up instructions on page 69.

(IMPORTANT NOTE: The game will continue dynamically as the demo progresses; new piñata will visit the garden, some piñata may even fight with each other. It is not necessary to get involved in any of these events and all speech from characters can be skipped by pressing 'Back'.)

Activity

Begin the activity by discussing a contentious issue that the pupils will feel strongly about (e.g. people dumping rubbish near schools/pollution). While discussing this topic, encourage pupils to be persuasive, and list effective examples of sentences for the pupils to refer back to in their writing task.

Watch the opening cinematic of the game. (This loads automatically when the new garden is selected from the menu.) The cinematic is fully voice-acted, with subtitles included. It may be necessary to re-watch the cinematic and this can be done as follows:

✿ Press *Start* when the player has full control of the game (after Seedos is introduced).

✿ Move the left directional stick down to the large red X and press A. Press A again on the large green tick to confirm.

✿ Once the game loads, complete the game set-up again to load a new garden.

When the clip has been sufficiently viewed, explain to the pupils that their task is to write a letter to Professor Pester, persuading him to leave the piñata alone.

As a class, generate a list of reasons why the Professor should leave the piñata alone. These may include:

✿ The piñata deserve the right to live without fear of being hunted.

✿ The piñata do not harm humans. So why should they be attacked?

✿ Piñatas make children across the world happy. Hunting them and capturing them would make children upset.

Once the list has been compiled, the success criteria for effective persuasive writing should be considered:

✿ Introduce the letter by clearly stating why you are writing (your viewpoint).

✿ Organise your supporting argument into paragraphs, mention the most powerful supporting argument first.

✿ Conclude the letter in a manner which makes your viewpoint clear.

✿ Use present tense.

✿ Use general statements to support views (Many piñata experts agree...).

✿ Use emotive language to persuade the reader.

✿ Use rhetorical questions.

✿ Use the appropriate level of formality.

Discuss the appropriate level of formality for the letter and, where possible, show examples. Arrive at the conclusion that due to the fact that he is a professor, formal language should be used. Co-author a formal letter on a different subject, following the success criteria carefully.

Look at the activity sheet on the following page. The letter from Professor Pester provides additional background for the pupils as well as an example of appropriate layout. Pupils can take some of the points made and refute them. Encourage pupils to annotate the letter and allow pupils to use it as a starting point for their own letters.

Pupils then write a formal letter to Professor Pester persuading him to stop hunting and hurting piñata. Encourage pupils to refer to the letter and the success criteria.

When the letter is completed, a useful peer-assessment tool would be to allow for a hot-seating session, where pupils take on the role of Professor Pester. Othe pupils then read their letter to the pupil in the 'hot seat' and they will then decide whether or not they might change their mind, giving reasons.

74 Piñata University Way
Piñata Island
P1N ATA

Pupils of this school

I have recently heard that you are planning to meddle in my scheme to hunt down and steal piñata. Although you may think what you are doing is right, I firmly believe that eradicating the world of these pesky piñata is the only way to make me happy. Children have fun hitting them to find the sweets, but surely it is more important that I am happy? If I capture every piñata then I can have all the sweets for myself and I will not be allowing any silly children to stand in my way!

Those vile piñata do not have feelings. They merely stand around in a small worthless garden doing nothing but eating and making silly piñata noises. By hunting and killing all of the piñatas in the garden, I can sell the land and new factories can be built in the area. I am certain that you would agree that this would be a far better use of the land on Piñata Island.

I hope this letter has made you realise that the lives of the worthless piñata are unimportant. I feel that you should be tending to more important matters like your homework.

Yours faithfully

Prof. Pester

Professor Pester

Activity Sixteen: To create a non-fiction television documentary script based upon Viva Piñata

Target

Using the dynamic world of Viva Piñata, pupils create a nature documentary.

How long?

The demo has a 25 minute (approximate) time limit but can be replayed as many times as required.

Activity: 45-60 minutes

Equipment

❋ Xbox 360 console (including Hard Disk Drive)

❋ Viva Piñata: Trouble In Paradise Demo (needs to be downloaded before the lesson from the Xbox Live Marketplace. See page 7.)

❋ Projector

❋ Drawing materials

Group size

Whole-class activity

Paired Work

Concept

Using the game, pupils create a documentary which they plan, write and perform orally. Before this lesson it will be necessary for pupils to have watched a nature documentary as a precursor to their own writing.

Game set-up

Follow the game set-up instructions on page 69.

(IMPORTANT NOTE: The game will continue dynamically as the demo progresses; new piñata will visit the garden, some piñata may even fight with each other. It is not necessary to get involved in any of these events and all speech from characters can be skipped by pressing Back.)

Activity

Discuss the key features of a play script. Generate a list of these. Do animal documentaries need a script? Discuss responses and arrive at the conclusion that a script is a necessary element. Explain that in this session pupils will be creating their own nature documentary based on the wild piñata of Piñata Island.

What are the key areas that will need to be considered for the documentary script?

✹ Camera (movement, zoom etc.)

✹ Spoken word (with expression)

✹ Location choices

✹ Timings

Load up the *Viva Piñata: Trouble in Paradise* demo as described previously. Invite one pupil to control the game and one pupil to be a speaker. During this activity the pupil controlling the game and the speaker will move the controller around, and tell the group what is going on in as much detail as they can. The rest of the group need access to drawing materials (e.g. whiteboards) and need to **sit with their backs facing the screen**. While the speaker is describing the scene (using the vocabulary prompts on the page overleaf, if needed) the other pupils will draw what they visualise to be happening on screen. Allow a short amount of time for this activity. As a group, discuss the drawings and the importance of using clear, descriptive dialogue.

As a group, create a documentary scene, with the teacher modelling the writing. Follow the conventions of a script so that pupils can see the correct layout of the text. Encourage the pupil in control of the game to use all of the features available (e.g. zoom) and explore the area fully. The piñata also give visual clues to feelings they may have (for example, they may be scared of another piñata in which case an exclamation mark will appear above their head along with a small picture of the animal they are afraid of.) This can be used to help add depth to the script.

Here is a sample section of a script:

Commentator: *(excited)* Look at that fantastic Pengum!

(Camera zooms in on the Pengum)

Commentator: Watch as he glides along the water elegantly.

(Camera follows Pengum as he moves towards his home.)

Commentator: The Pengum now, exhausted, returns to his home upon the icy ground.

Once a sample script has been written, the pupils can now create their own documentary. Grouped in pairs, success criteria should be made clear. (This can be adapted to suit the age/ability of the pupils.)

✻ Name of speaker in margin

✻ Directions in brackets

✻ Directions in present tense

✻ Adverbs used to instruct the commentator

✻ Clear, descriptive language

✻ Technical and specific vocabulary

✻ Generalisations used for effect

Due to the dynamic nature of the game and the important fact that pupils are in control, a dynamic script should be created. As the writing is underway, encourage pupils to think carefully about the directions given:

✻ Where do you want your documentary to begin?

✻ Where do you want your documentary to end?

✻ Which key piñata are you going to focus on?

✻ Is the description of the key events gripping?

Pupils may need to spend time on the game to help with their writing. This can be structured so that every pair has a turn. Other pupils will need to work on planning their script before accessing the demo.

When the task is completed, invite pairs to perform their script, one pupil controlling the game and the other reading the script. Both pupils will need to take care to follow the written directions. Teachers may wish to record these performances as a form of assessment. At the end of each performance, peer-assessment can be used to discuss the directions and dialogue used.

Some sentence starters to get the ball rolling:

It is truly amazing...

If you look...

Here we can see...

Although not uncommon...

Ah yes, here is the...

Behind the ....

Swimming expertly...

To the left of...

To the right of...

Above the...

Below the...

Watch closely as the...

During the day the...

If we look closely...

Friday 26th February
L.o To write an encyclopaedia entry pinata

Name: The Bullbottle

where it lives (habbilat).
The Bullbottle's habbitat is in the lacklala
beach wich has sugary sands and cola seas.
Both female and mait male live there and its also
suprising that there not extinct because they are
rare to find.

what it looks likes
The male species are a range of black white and
blue where on the other hand the females
are a viriaty of colous exept from red (becase
they hate the colour red and they get vexed.)
They have two horns on the top of thers head
and the more bigger the horns are the more
cooler they are.

What they eat.
The Bullbottle particully eats blue candy canes
wich both species eat.
The Bullbottle – that eats candy canes – turns candy
canes into cola bottles.
The speciman of the male produces normal cola
bottles however the females produce different
coloured cola bottles.

<u>likes and dislikes</u>
The Bullbottle likes many things such as: flowers,
a lot of company; being liked and blue.
The Bull-bottle hate the colour red, pub
and red by it and it will get very vexed and
it also hate fruit and veg.

This lesson was great I had fun
making it up. ☺

NOTES

NOTES

NOTES

EFFECTIVE
SCHOOL BASED
TRAINING
FOR ALL STAFF

Alan runs school-based training on Literacy and Thinking Skills

Prices start at **£975 + VAT** (plus **£85** towards local accommodation, the night prior to the event, plus 'at cost' travelling expenses) for a single school.

For **two** schools clustering the price drops to **£750** per school and for **three** schools to **£675** per school.

For larger numbers fees are negotiated directly with Alan.

IF SCHOOLS WISH TO SELL OUT ADDITIONAL PLACES TO OFFSET COSTS WE ASK THAT THEY CHARGE NO MORE THAN £95 PER PLACE. We add an additional £55 for each place 'sold on' and the school retains £40.

To book a place either call
07789938923
or email
alanpeat@tiscali.co.uk

Visit www.alanpeat.com for further information

Buy Alan's books from www.thecepress.com

**50 Ways to Retell a Story:
Cinderella**
by Alan Peat, Julie Peat
& Christopher Storey

**Get Your Head Around
Punctuation
(and how to teach it)**
by Alan Peat

**Writing Exciting Sentences
Age 7 Plus**
by Alan Peat

**Improving Non-fiction Writing
at Key Stage 1 & 2:
The Success Approach**
by Margaret McNeil
& Alan Peat

**Improving Story Writing
at Key Stage 1 & 2**
by Alan Peat

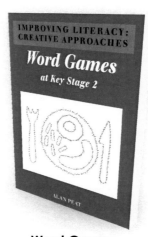

**Word Games
at Key Stage 2**
by Alan Peat

**Teaching Poetry
with 7 - 12 year olds**
by Alan Peat

**Teaching Poetry
with 4 - 8 year olds**
by Alan Peat

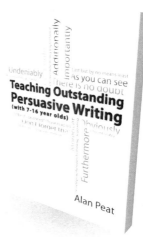

**Teaching Outstanding
Persuasive Writing**
by Alan Peat